The Book of Prayer of Sor María of Santo Domingo

Sancta cruz dela magdalena.

The Book of Prayer of Sor María of Santo Domingo

A Study and Translation

Mary E. Giles

State University of New York Press

Published by
State University of New York Press, Albany

Printed in the United States of America

For information, address State University of New York Press, State University Plaza, Albany, N.Y., 12246

Library of Congress Cataloging-in-Publication Data

Giles, Mary E.
The book of prayer of Sor María of Santo Domingo : a study and translation / Mary E. Giles.
p. cm.
Bibliography: p.
Includes index.
ISBN 0-7914-0235-5. — ISBN 0-7914-0236-3 (pbk.)
1. María de Santo Domingo, sor, 16 cent. 2. Dominicans—Spain—Biography. 3. María de Santo Domingo, sor, 16th cent. Libro de la oración. 4. Spirituality. I. Maria de Santo Domingo, sor, 16th cent. Libro de la oración. English. 1989. II. Title.
BX4705.M3272G55 1990
271'.97202—dc20
[B] 89-11578
CIP

10 9 8 7 6 5 4 3 2 1

Contents

Foreword

Although Sor María of Santo Domingo and Teresa of Ávila are women of the sixteenth century who came from the same general area of Spain, they did not know each other personally. By the year 1515 when Teresa was born, Sor María had already experienced the ambiguous rewards of fame; her reputation as a visionary woman of extraordinary gifts had brought her to the courts of princes of state and Church but it had also thrust her into a painful series of interrogations by Church officials. Yet, when I consider the spectrum of religious and cultural life of sixteenth-century Spain, I see Sor María and Teresa in much the same light: both aspired to lives of intense devotion to the Crucified Christ while extending themselves outward to reform religious practice.

There are, of course, enormous spiritual differences between the holy woman of Piedrahita and the saint from Ávila that explain why the one has been a relatively minor figure in Christian history whereas the other plays a principal role as reformer, writer, saint and doctor of the Catholic church. In my mind, however, the women are linked, in part because of their similar intentions and accomplishments and in part because it was my love for Teresa and desire to understand her better that directed me to the early years of her century, when men and women planted the seeds of religious reform that she later would nourish to fruition.

What started as a research project for one year stretched into three years and will continue for many more as the literature I find myself investigating turns out to be far richer, more complex and engaging than I had anticipated. I was especially intrigued by the documented appearance of religious and secular women as teachers, prophets and spiritual guides in the innovative religious movements of the first thirty-five years of the century. At the same time I was fascinated, though less happily so, by records of the Inquisition whose lists of people examined by the tribunal included woman after woman identified with only the phrase "wife of so-and-so." Who were these women, I wondered, and what had they done to warrant interrogation by the Inquisition? What did it really mean to be charged with witchcraft or heresy or immorality? And how could I pull away the mask of anonymity to meet the woman of flesh and blood?

I was especially sensitive to the anonymous women because studies about women whose identities and records are known suggest that their "crimes" are remarkably similar to the actions of Christian feminists today who confront the sexism of the Christian Church in ministries that are officially or unofficially sanctioned. If my sympathies lie with Sor María of Santo Domingo, it is because on a personal level she reminds me that each woman in her own way and her own time answers the call to live as a unique human being and that we as scholars must try to meet her on these, her own, terms.

The existence of Sor María and the relatively recent discovery of her *Book of Prayer* (1948) are further encouragement for scholars to persist in the search for women's names and faces and texts. Women's spirituality of sixteenth—century Spain is a story that is just beginning to be written and one that will require the on-going dedication of many scholars before we can cast the major and minor female characters in the unfolding drama of Christianity and discern the significance of newly emerging lines of action.

Aware of the important research yet to be done on the general subject of women's spirituality in Spain and specifically on Sor María, I view this study and translation of her *Book* as only an introduction to the woman, her times and her text; others will continue the urgent work of preparing a critical edition of the Spanish text, comparing her to other visionary women in and out of Spain, and analyzing the ecstatic text from the point of view of semiotics.

The reader will note that Spanish names which are familiar in their anglicized spelling are left as such: Queen Isabel, King Ferdinand, Teresa of Ávila and John of the Cross. Other spellings of proper names retain the Spanish rendering.

There are several people whose assistance I would like to acknowledge. William C. Bryant's work in reading the translation has been invaluable; in polishing the final phrasing in English, he and I have also polished a friendship that goes back to our days in graduate school. Further notes of gratitude go to: Robert Boenig and Paul McGinnis for English translations of passages in Latin; Jodi Bilinkoff for sharing her own research on Sor María; Marijane Osborn for insights into the dramatic aspects of Sor María's contemplations; William Sullivan, dean of the School of Arts and Sciences, and the Committee on Research, both of California State University, Sacramento, for grants that provided time for research for the book; William Eastman and the editorial staff of the State University of New York Press for their help in transforming a manuscript into a book.

Part I

The Study

Introduction

"I have heard of a new type of worship springing up," wrote Peter Martyr to the Count of Tendilla. It was, he explained, a woman from Piedrahita who claimed to be a prophet.[1] The celebrated Italian humanist devoted the remainder of his October 6, 1509 letter to news of the holy woman who called herself the bride of Christ, conversed with her Spouse and the Blessed Mother in ecstasy, and fasted so rigorously that she could scarcely hold food in her stomach. In words uttered while stretched out rigid in ecstasy, in the form of Christ Crucified, the illiterate woman was said to rival theologians in her wisdom. But, Peter Martyr advised, opinion was sharply divided about the holy woman. "It is a matter of debate," he wrote, "whether they [ecstasies] are trifles or the outpourings of an inspired mind." Although her own Dominicans could not agree if she was blessed or a superstition that ought to be extirpated, everyone agreed that she enjoyed favor in high places; the king himself, "who is of sound mind," thought her manifestations genuine in spirit, while Spain's foremost prelate, Cardinal Cisneros, "argued that divine wisdom was poured into her." Not even their favor could still the debate that finally forced the pontiff to action; he named a commission to examine the matter and, he hoped, ward off the scandal that would erupt if the affair turned out to be nothing but female hysteria. As for Peter Martyr, time, he concluded, was the truest judge.

The center of the controversy was an uneducated peasant woman from the monastery of Santo Domingo in the town of Piedrahita near Ávila. Chronicles refer to her as Sor María of Santo Domingo or the Beata of Piedrahita. The term *beata* means a holy or blessed woman and it appears in records of the middle of the fifteenth century to designate a woman who quits the world and alone or in a small community with other women lives in prayer and on public charity. At that time beatas may simply have been women who fashioned a spiritual life of their own because they could not pay the dowries required for admittance to the feminine convents.[2] By the end of the fifteenth century, when the establishment of new convents and tertiaries provided more spiritual options for women, the term beata referred not only to women who individually or in groups "chose an informal religious vocation as beatas"[3] but also to women such as Sor María who joined a third order.[4]

The commission named by the pope heard Sor María's case in the winter of 1509–10. Not only did the examiners exonerate her of all charges, but they praised her devout, exemplary life.[5] Their approval came as no surprise since King Ferdinand and Cardinal Cisneros had a hand in selecting the examiners. Not even the weight of their positive judgment could suppress controversy about the Beata. In a letter dated June 26, 1512 Peter Martyr repeated much of what he had previously said about the Beata—that in ecstasy her limbs were rigid as tree trunks and in conversation she addressed the Blessed Mother as mother-in-law because she, the Beata, was mystically espoused with Jesus—but he also updated news of the woman from Piedrahita. In spite of the favorable outcome of the proceedings, he wrote, debate still raged between the Beata's critics and her advocates who praised her sanctity to the stars ("sanctitatem ejus extollunt ad sidera").[6] The unsettled state of affairs seems to have affected Peter Martyr's own writing, for he closes with the words, "now enough going round and round about this blessed little girl."

Even though Sor María no longer appeared ecstasized before the king and cardinal as she had prior to the examination, word of her extraordinary behavior went out from the monastery where a skeptical master general of the Dominican Order, Thomas Cajetan, had ordered her to remain.

From the silence of the monastery Sor María herself became the battle cry for rigorist-minded brothers of Piedrahita who championed the austerities of a Savonarola-inspired reform even if it meant secession from the order. When this internal conflict finally subsided about three years after the examination of Sor María, so also did controversy about her. From chronicles of the time as well as later ones, the Beata appears to have lived quietly as foundress-abbess of a generously endowed monastery in Aldeanueva until her death around 1524, her reputation as a devout, virtuous woman intact.[7]

Not only are Peter Martyr's letters an invaluable account by a reasonable bystander, but they are also the primary source of information about Sor María for early historians. Álvaro Gómez de Castro relied on the humanist's letters in his biography of Cardinal Cisneros as did Lorenzo Galíndez de Carvajal in his history of the Catholic Kings.[8] When historians such as Juan Antonio Llorente and Henry Charles Lea investigated the Spanish Inquisition in the nineteenth century, they also turned to Peter Martyr's writings for information on this woman whom they associated with the *alumbrados* (enlightened ones), men and women in and around Toledo whose practices and teachings were pronounced heretical in 1525. The wording of Lea's account, in which he identifies Sor María as the first of the beatas to be identified with the *alumbrados*, is reminiscent of Peter Martyr:

> The daughter of a fanatic peasant, she had been carefully trained in mystic exercises and was wholly given up to contemplative abstraction, in which she enjoyed the most intimate relations with God, in whose arms she was dissolved in love. Sometimes she asserted that Christ was with her, sometimes that she was Christ herself or the bride of Christ; often she held conversations with the Virgin in which she spoke for both. As her reputation spread, her visions and revelations won for her the character of a prophetess.[9]

Lea's biases are clear; noting that she was exonerated of charges, he concludes that "such success naturally stimulated imitation and was the foreshadowing of wide-spread delusion and imposture."[10]

The most incriminating remarks about Sor María are in a study of Spanish heterodoxy by the eminent nineteenth-century scholar, Menéndez Pelayo. Perhaps more than any other scholar, Menéndez Pelayo was responsible for casting Sor María's lot with the heretical *alumbrados.* "Tales of miracles and deceptions were not rare cases," comments Menéndez Pelayo about the early years of the sixteenth century, and the Beata of Piedrahita is one of the "oldest examples of which we have evidence."[11] "She was not a vicious woman," he continues, "but fanatic, yes, and enlightened." Menéndez Pelayo uses the word *iluminada* (enlightened) to mean that Sor María was heretical in the sense that *alumbrados* were: they relied on the infused light of the Holy Spirit to the exclusion of the sacraments and external works of devotion. He also attributed her exoneration to the influence of powerful protectors, adding to her further discredit that the examiners "did not dare to decide if the spirit that spoke in that woman was celestial or diabolical."[12]

Although Manuel Serrano y Sanz in his dictionary of Spanish women authors, published in 1915, was more charitable than either Lea or Menéndez Pelayo in that he did not classify the Beata as an *alumbrada,* the biases are nonetheless unmistakable. She became famous, he says, "for the divine favors she claimed to receive," and was absolved in the proceedings "thanks to the influence of high people and because she seemed deluded rather than heresiarch or deceptive."[13]

Few scholars, with the exception of Emilio Colunga, writing in a series of articles in *Ciencia Tomista* from 1914 to 1916, took issue with the biased methodology of historians like Menéndez Pelayo who assumed that the work of the Inquisition was right and necessary and out of hand accepted its judgments and attitudes as the absolute measure of the individuals under its jurisdiction. Emilio Colunga questioned

Menéndez Pelayo's credentials for making the judgments he did, maintaining in his discussion of the *alumbrados* that the distinguished scholar "lacked the necessary theological preparation to treat these questions properly." He further said that "since these are subtle, complex questions, Sr. Menéndez Pelayo deceives himself if he believes that the good judgment and catechetical instruction every Christian should have is enough for judging the propositions of Carranza."[14]

Since about 1940 scholarship has shown signs of restlessness under the accumulated weight of prejudice. The reasoned approach of Marcel Bataillon in his benchmark study of Erasmus and Spain[15] not only gave enormous impetus to the study of religion and spirituality in the first decades of the sixteenth century but also opened the door to a rehabilitation of the *alumbrados* and other suspicious types like the Beata of Piedrahita. With a veritable flowering of studies on the subject of the *alumbrados,* a rehabilitation has taken place in terms of their importance for understanding the social and spiritual climate of this significiant period of Spanish history as well as a desire to identify and value as real human beings the men and women masked by biases and inadequate documentation.

Splendid books and articles abound on the development of illuminism in the sixteenth and seventeenth centuries and on major figures such as Francisca Hernández, María de Cazalla, Isabel de la Cruz and Pedro Ruiz de Alcaraz.[16] This surge of interest in the spirituality of the early sixteenth century and a revision of methodology in the direction of more open inquiry have encouraged a fresh look at the Beata of Piedrahita. In an informative polemic that extended through several articles, the Dominican Vicente Beltrán de Heredia and the Jesuit Bernardino Llorca tackled the question of whether the Beata even was an *alumbrada.* For Heredia, the Beata is a pivotal figure in the reform movement within the Spanish Dominican Order, a subject on which he is the recognized authority, while the Jesuit polemicist sees her significance relative to the *alumbrados.* Regardless of the larger frame of their studies, both scholars focus on the Beata in a clear, compelling manner.

The importance that both Heredia and Llorca claimed for Sor María was underscored in 1948 when a manuscript was discovered in the archives of the University of Zaragoza and published in a facsimile edition, with study, by José Manuel Blecua.[17] The manuscript contained a collection of Sor María's writings, or rather the written form of what she said in ecstasy and dictated out of ecstasy, along with a summary of her life and other explanatory material written by an unidentified editor. Internal evidence from the text proves that the book was published several years after the 1509–10 examination of the Beata; one scholar sets the date between 1517 and 1522, with 1518 the most likely year.[18]

Entitled *The Book of Prayer of Sor María of Santo Domingo,* the little volume, together with a few letters, a miscellaneous fragment of her revelations, and her testimony as recorded in the documents of the examination, constitute a first-hand perspective on an illiterate rustic woman whose devotion caused such scandal that a prince of state and a prince of the Church rushed to her defense. Not surprisingly, the discovery of this material raises new questions as well as sharpening some old ones and resolving others. The *Book* ought to clear the air of lingering charges that Sor María was the first in a line of beatas to embrace heretical illuminist teachings. Moreover, the text, by the fact of its existence, urges further investigation into the relationship of Sor María and the Dominican Order and the role of beatas in the religious life of sixteenth-century Spain.

The fact of the *Book* as text generates intriguing questions: What does it mean to compose in ecstasy? How does one evaluate the artistry of ecstatic writing? Was Sor María an "author" even though she did not write down her words? Finally, given the additional evidence about Sor María that the *Book* yields, was she a mystic of the order of a Catherine of Siena or a Teresa of Ávila? And what place ought she to occupy in the spiritual story of women in and out of Spain? This range of questions informs the following chapters on the life, character, teachings and times of Sor María of Santo Domingo, the Beata of Piedrahita.

Chapter One

Sor María: Her Life and Examination

Publication of both Sor María's *Book of Prayer* and the documents of her examination, as well as the superb studies by Vicente Beltrán de Heredia and Bernardino Llorca, have added significant new information about the Beata that consequently enhances our understanding of her motives and aspirations. Nonetheless, much of her life remains a puzzle, beginning with her date of birth. Serrano y Sanz fixes the date between 1470 and 1475; Heredia decides on 1486; José Manuel Blecua does not state a preference in citing both dates.[1] There is agreement that she was born in Aldeanueva in the district of Barco de Ávila, not far from the well-known town of Ávila. Little is known about her parents, who were humble, illiterate laborers, though her father is referred to as a religious fanatic and a seventeenth-century account connects her mother with the family of the Paniaguas in Ávila. To their credit, from the point of view of Sor María's defenders in the investigation, her parents were true Christian and Catholic folk who were always held in good esteem and clear of any suspicion that they might be descended from Jews or heretics.[2]

The proceedings of the examination disclose the portrait of an exceptionally religious little girl. One witness recalled hearing an elderly cleric who had known Sor María since childhood tell of difficult fasts, abstinences and penitence and the girl's custom of disciplining herself to the point of bleeding. Virtues blossomed in the child who regularly confessed and received communion beyond the times prescribed by the Church and who gave alms to the poor even though she herself was impoverished. In short, she was a marvel to all who knew her.

By Heredia's calculations, Sor María was seventeen when she received the habit of a third order Dominican at the monastery of Santo in the town of Piedrahita near Aldeanueva. She lived in their residence for lay sisters until May 28, 1504 when she entered the lay house of Santa Catalina in Ávila. By the spring of 1507 she had left Santa Catalina and transferred to the Dominican monastery of Santo Tomás, which was also in Ávila. There is reason to believe that she had to leave Santa Catalina because of disagreements with other religious women in the house, although she and her supporters later testified that the move was to escape persecution.[3]

In October of 1507, Sor María was on the road with men and women friends bound for Toledo, where she was bent on instituting in the Dominican houses there the reforms for which she and her supporters were already famous.[4] In a letter of October 18th, the provincial of the order, Diego Magdaleno, had granted requests from the prior of Salamanca and his companion, Father Juan Hurtado de Mendoza, authorizing the Beata to promote stricter observance, especially in matters of fast, abstinence and penance.

Sor María's program for reform did not meet unflagging enthusiasm. Not only were such reforms unpalatable to many Dominicans in Toledo, but the Beata herself was controversial for what they deemed to be extravagant behavior on her part. Her public raptures and prophecies were particularly offensive when she praised the Inquisition in ecstasy and maligned the *conversos* (the converted ones, referring to Christians of Jewish or Moslem descent) who were numerous and influential in Toledo's population.

The incident that apparently brought the affair of Sor María to the attention of higher officials in the Church and state had to do with her ecstasies and the *conversos*.[5] Perhaps the *conversos* whom she had offended with her ecstatic remarks had determined to take their revenge by calling into question the genuineness of her raptures. The story told later by a witness at the investigation is that when she had taken up residence at a Dominican house for brothers, she was ordered to receive communion in a chapel of the church, which she did, although unwillingly. The order originated in a request from some devout women as well as other people who did not care for the Beata; presumably they were *conversos*. These people must have wanted to observe the Beata receiving communion so that they could get evidence she was feigning the raptures that usually overtook her at communion. The result was that they did observe her and they did complain to both King Ferdinand and Cardinal Cisneros who were in Burgos at the time.

Meanwhile Sor María had incurred the enmity of the Provincial Magdaleno when in the state of rapture she had threatened him if he did not push for the reforms that she advocated. Her threats exacerbated the doubts that he already had about her reputed holiness, for when he had observed her in Toledo she seemed neither very prayerful nor very humble.

Whatever the nature of the criticism about Sor María, it was serious enough to warrant intervention by the king. On November 26, 1507, King Ferdinand wrote Magdaleno instructing him to come to Burgos, where the court was in residence, and to bring with him Diego de Vitoria, prior of Santo Tomás of Ávila and confessor to Sor María. He was ordered to make haste and make sure that the Beata, who was still in Toledo, return to her monastery in Ávila until further notice.

Magdaleno and Vitoria answered the king's call immediately. The outcome of their conversation with the monarch was another summons, this one to Sor María, who thus found herself in the winter of 1507–08 at court in Burgos and the center of attention. She was famous for her public raptures and even went into trance on request, as it were, once in the presence of the queen of Aragón and the lady Juana of Aragón. Not only was she said to be enraptured on request but her ecstasies even marked the canonical hours: she was said to have been enraptured in the morning at the hour of prime rather than matins so as to accommodate the schedule of a certain lady.

Such phenomena did not escape notice by Cardinal Cisneros, the primate of Spain and a theological and political figure of enormous consequence. Sor María did not disappoint the cardinal when she appeared at his request in Santa María de Nieva. He confided to Hurtado that he had never seen living doctrine until he beheld Sor María. His faith in her went so far that he charged Diego Vitoria to write down her ecstatic utterances and send them to him for his own spiritual edification.

So favorable was her reception by both the king and cardinal that Sor María and her followers set in motion plans for a new monastery of religious women in Aldeanueva; among the recruits were two of Sor María's sisters, known in the convent as María de la Asunción and María de los Santos. By this time a third man had entered the ranks of the Beata's supporters to form with the king and Cisneros a formidable triumvirate on her behalf. Fadrique Álvarez of Toledo, the powerful duke of Alba, was so pleased to have in his vicinity—he had jurisdiction over the area of Valdecorneja from 1485 to 1531—a person of Sor María's reputed sanctity that he offered to underwrite the expense of a new foundation. Work began immediately. During its construction Sor María lived in Piedrahita and Barco de Ávila, thus giving rise to speculation among historians that there might have been two beatas, one in Piedrahita and the other in Barco de Ávila. Most scholars, however, discount the theory of two beatas.[6]

The favor that Sor María enjoyed with her prestigious admirers did not quench the flames of controversy that by early 1508 threatened schism in the Spanish Dominican Order. She and the rigorous observance she promoted in the monasteries were the manifest topic of debate at the February 1508 chapter meeting in Zamora. Sor María was present, summoned, her critics said, because of the scandal she caused and not, as her confessor would maintain, to show her off, though by that time, a witness later said, Vitoria was afraid to attend the chapter and be seen with the Beata lest he offend Magdaleno whose attitude toward Sor María had turned chilly.[7] Father Antonio de Benavente testified that he heard Vitoria was afraid to see her; when told he would not see her again, she replied that he was to hear her confession, give her communion and return with her to the monastery—which he did. In spite of his fear of the provincial, Vitoria attended the chapter a few days after Sor María had.

There is clear evidence that the majority of those in attendance did not support Sor María. Two of the definitors explicitly opposed the Beata; six of nine ordinances passed were directed against the reformers. In the matter of dress, for example, they prohibited excesses in the direction of either the overly wide, long garments favored by the conventuals or the observants' narrow, shorter habit adopted from the usage of Savonarola and the Congregation of St. Mark in Italy. The ordinance authorizing the use of woolen mattresses, according to provisions in the rules in provinces where the observance was in effect, and prohibiting superiors from imposing mortifications other than those detailed in the constitution was an obvious refutation of the Beata's recommendation that the brothers and sisters should sleep on a board as she did. In general the ordinances prohibited innovations unless approved by the provincial chapter, even in matters that had authorization through apostolic letters. Two ordinances were directed personally at the Beata and her reform-minded followers. The one that declared members excommunicated from the order if they sought support from people other than Dominicans was intended for Antonio de la Peña who, as preacher for the king, frequented the court and persuaded Cisneros to use his power to discharge and name superiors in the order. The other ordinance struck sharply at the Beata: no religious person could meet with Sor María or even write her without written permission from the provincial for each occasion.[8]

Sor María's supporters reacted defiantly to the ordinances. In bold refutation of the ordinance that prohibited political manuevering outside the order, they turned to dependable support, asking the king and Cisneros to appeal to the master general of the order in Rome, Thomas Cajetan. The effort was successful; on March 4, 5 and 6 of 1508, Cajetan issued three dispositions to the province, the third of which charged

Francisco de Porres (who would replace Magdaleno as provincial by Cajetan's order of June 29, 1508) with investigating the matter of Sor María and her extraordinary phenomena. The disposition reached Spain in April.

In the meantime, Sor María on the advice of her confessor, Vitoria, and assured of support from the king, the cardinal, and the duke, proceeded with her tasks as foundress while her male advocates in the order frankly rebelled against the ordinance about securing written permission for each conversation or correspondence with the Beata. It appears that the reformers went on their way as if the chaper meeting of February had not taken place, though not without incurring rumor and gossip.

By the end of April, Magdaleno acted. To obtain more information about Sor María in preparation for the next chapter meeting, he sent the prior of Ávila, Domingo de Santa Cruz, to Aldeanueva, where he met not only opposition from the Beata's defenders but imprisonment as well. Claiming that Francisco de Porres had been charged with examining the matter of Sor María, her allies confined him in a small jail where he remained until the following summer when a new provincial, Tomás de Matienzo, ordered his release. From the beginning, Matienzo had been favorable to Sor María; thus, in September of 1508, when he himself traveled to Piedrahita, he put in charge of an investigation none other than Diego de Vitoria, the Beata's confessor and her colleague in the reform movement. Both Heredia and Llorca designate this investigation of September as the first in a series of four. As Llorca notes, we have no special notice of the results of this first examination, but undoubtedly it was entirely favorable to Sor María.[9]

The affair did not end with one proceeding; three more were to follow before resolving the internal conflict that was pushing the order toward schism. Magdaleno continued to agitate for action against the reformers and their holy woman. Finally, in December of 1508, Cajetan asked the archbishop of Seville, Diego de Deza, and the bishop of Burgos, Pascual de Ampudia, both Dominicans, to examine Sor María and put an end to the disagreeable business.

Sor María was ordered to obey the judges; all religious of the province were to tell the examiners everything they knew about the woman, good and bad; under pain of excommunication Diego de Vitoria was to report all facts about the Beata and what she said, and furthermore he was to appear before the general. If the judgment of the examiners was to strip Sor María of her religious habit and prohibit her living in a Dominican house, then no one was to admit her; if, on the other hand, they agreed she was to remain in a convent of nuns, then the women were to accept and care for her until the matter was fully resolved. This, the second of the four proceedings, was not allowed to take place.

Magdaleno had not been waiting silently in the wings. Disillusioned with Cajetan, Magdaleno had gone to the top, persuading Pope Julius II to take action. With the naming of three apostolic judges, Cajetan's commission was terminated. The new judges were Alonso de Fonseca, the archbishop of Santiago and patriarch of Alexandria, Alfonso Carrillo de Albornoz, bishop of Ávila, and Pascual de Ampudia, bishop of Burgos and also a member of the two-man commission named by Cajetan.

Sor María's supporters were unhappy with the membership of the tribunal; they were suspicious of Fonseca's intentions and convinced that the bishop of Burgos was biased against the Beata. Nonetheless, the wheels of the investigation began turning shortly after the brief that commissioned the process arrived in Spain, probably around the end of May 1509. Sor María, her associates and witnesses were instructed to appear in Salamanca, where Fonseca was. At this time Sor María was at the height of her popularity, the subject of many extraordinary phenomena, and allegedly God's instrument for prophecy.[10] It was soon apparent, however, that the work of the tribunal boded ill for Sor María. As before, her defenders were quick to mount an attack.

No sooner did Sor María's advocates sense a hostile wind than they instituted action to subvert the tribunal. Shortly before Matienzo was to leave office, he appealed to Rome to name a new tribunal which would be favorable to the Beata. He had to act swiftly if he was to be successful; Agustín de Funes had been elected provincial in June and Matienzo had only until the end of the month before confirmation of Funes's election would reach Spain and end his chances to support the Beata. Diego de Vitoria presented the appeal, dated June 13, 1509, to the licentiate Francisco de Herrera in Valladolid. The basis of the appeal was that the party requesting the brief to charge the judges with examining Sor María was not disinterested but prejudicial to her legitimate religious superior. The appeal went immediately to Rome and Matienzo named attorneys to communicate it to the judges who, throughout these legal stirrings, were proceeding with their investigation of the Beata.

On July 21, 1509 the mayor of Salamanca, Juan de Ovalle, ordered the judges to suspend proceedings because their biases against Sor María invalidated their appointment. He said that if the pope had been advised of the degree of their animosity, it was unlikely he would have granted them the brief. Moreover, it had come to Ovalle's attention that Alonso de Fonseca had often called Sor María a great folly and asserted that were she under his jurisdiction she would receive her deserved punishment. Furthermore, he had heard that the bishop of Burgos had said, among other nasty things, that whoever followed Sor María was a heretic, that he would burn her and her sympathizers, and that even if the king did not desire it, he, as bishop of Burgos, would continue investigation into the affairs of the Beata and her collaborators.

Before the judges replied to the mayor, news reached Spain that on July third, Cajetan had verified the confirmation of Agustín de Funes as provincial, thus ending the authority of Matienzo and his delegate, Diego de Vitoria. Now the judges responded in force to Juan de Ovalle; they totally rejected the authority of Matienzo and his delegate, Vitoria, who was acting as the Beata's defense counsel. Their investigation, which was the third of the proceedings, went forward but was never completed.

Into the by-then raging battle rushed fresh troops from the Beata's side, in the guise of a new brief from the pope, dated July 16, 1509, which disbanded the existent tribunal, entrusted the papal nuncio Juan Rulfo with the examination of Sor María, and authorized the king to assist in the proceedings. The king responded by naming to the tribunal his Dominican confessor, Juan de Enguera, bishop of Vich and inquisitor general of Aragón.

The nuncio received the brief on August eighteenth and immediately communicated its contents to the three-person tribunal, which was still at work on Sor María's case. Informed on the twenty-seventh of that month, the bishop of Ávila complied with the instruction to terminate the proceedings, as did Fonseca, but the bishop of Burgos, who had received the notice in Palencia on the twenty-third, was not so easily set aside. Three days later he denounced the means by which the brief had been obtained through the king's intervention and advised His Holiness that by right they ought to protest one, two and three times and inform him about the details of this business that have occurred and are occurring and what they are like: "And how we say it and respond and protest, we ask the present notary to advise us."[11]

Thus were the murky beginnings of the last and fourth examination, whose proceedings have been conserved in part to provide a window onto a bizarre scene of battle. This is the investigation that Peter Martyr mentions in his letter of October sixth, written only three days after the Beata had received in Aldeanueva the order to appear before the two-man tribunal in Valladolid. Although Peter Martyr has some of the details confused, such as combining the third and fourth examinations into one with a panel that erroneously included the bishop of Burgos, he appears to have caught the mood of the affair; the Beata was the news of the day and the fact that both the king and Cisneros were interested parties added spice to the talk. Of their interest in the Beata there is no doubt whatsoever. Cisneros, who was not in Valladolid when the examination began, wrote from Alcalá de Henares to the nuncio on October twenty-ninth:

> I know that this business of Sor María has been entrusted to you by his Holiness, and I am very pleased about it since

> he thereby may be the judge of this case. And because it affects so much the honor of a very great and outstanding Order, I especially beseech you to consider it with all the caution and maturity that is appropriate and which he expects. And what I feel about this business and can tell you is that this religious woman has seemed like an angelic person in all respects, and I have always seen her with infinite tears and other signs of great devotion and holiness. With respect to what they say about her saying that there was in Italy a person who was to reform the Church and other similar things, I can certify to you that I never heard her say anything like that when I spoke with her. And in such affairs as this people always say and bring up a thousand falsehoods. And although it is not necessary to urge him to be careful to consider and settle the affair as is appropriate, I did want to write to let him know my opinion and how I feel about the affair and entrust to him whatever I can since this is something that affects so much the service to our Lord.[12]

The examination of Sor María that took place in October, November and December of 1509 in Valladolid was not a formal inquisitorial proceeding. Controlled by Cisneros, the king and the duke of Alba, Enguera and the nuncio apparently did little more than ensure a favorable outcome for the Beata. Without a prosecuting attorney and with a defender (Antonio de la Peña) who was one of Sor María's fervent admirers, the examination has been called a sham; its outcome was so predictable that the Beata's adversaries withdrew from the proceedings in the realization that their case was hopeless.[13] Interestingly, the master general of the order continued to reproach the Beata for her behavior and curtailed her activities among the Dominicans.

Even though the examination was "rigged" and the witnesses whose testimony is available were generally well disposed to the Beata, the nature and seriousness of the accusations that provoked the multiple attempts to investigate Sor María can be discerned in the documents and need to be set forth. Here a sketch of the criticisms will suffice until further analysis in the next chapter.

The most serious criticisms of Sor María concerned the extraordinary phenomena and her behavior with male religious. Her critics had grave doubts about the genuineness of the raptures which overcame her frequently and with suspicious convenience. While enraptured, she was wont to converse with the Blessed Mother, the saints and Jesus himself, to utter prophecies on both secular and religious matters, and to answer questions on theology and sacred scripture, which those in attendance put to her. She was also famous for ecstatic communion in which she miraculously received the host without the priest giving it to her. She was customarily ecstasized at the time of the consecration whether or not she was physically present at the mass. Furthermore, she was reportedly a stigmatic; her side had first opened and bled on the eve of Holy Thursday in 1509.

The lengthiest testimony in the proceedings studied was offered by several men on behalf of her moral rectitude. She herself admitted to the examiners that her confessor spent nights alone with her, sometimes near her bed and at other times on top of it; she explained that he was there because she suffered problems with her heart and was terribly afraid of the devil, whose physical and spiritual torments she needed help to escape.[14] Many religious men visited the Beata in search of spiritual wisdom and edification, but the testimony shows that there was room for doubt concerning the honesty of intention or act on the part of some of the men, if not on hers.

There were objections to her dress and penchant for games and dances, questions about her rigorous fasts and frequent illnesses, and always hovering over the proceedings was the concern about her relationship with the order and especially the position she occupied in the plans of the brothers of Piedrahita. The monastery was showing a disturbing restlessness to get on with reform; the monks even seemed determined to institute a program of their own if the reform planned by the order was not to their liking.

The gathering of testimony concluded in December while the session was still in Valladolid. Antonio de la Peña gave two defenses, one after another, in which he responded to charges made in various proceedings. He was granted two months from the beginning of the next year to prove the demands that constituted the defenses. Then the tribunal moved to Madrid where the court had also transferred. At the end of February 1510, Antonio de la Peña was granted an extension of one month to gather proof and witnesses in favor of Sor María. Beltrán de Heredia explains that the extant documents of the proceeding contain only the allegations presented by the defender and portions of testimony given by the witnesses he called.[15]

Nearing the end of the examination, the nuncio invited Cardinal Cisneros and members of the Council of the Inquisition to form a tribunal with him and the bishop of Vich. Meeting in Madrid on March 23, 1510 they unanimously voted not merely to absolve Sor María of the charges but to commend her to God as a woman of holy life and behavior.[16] Three days later the sentence was published: the tribunal enumerated the allegations for and against the Beata in the various examinations; declared her intentions good and blameless; concluded that "her life and holiness are commendable and worthy and deserving of praise"; and imposed perpetual silence about the case on everyone.[17]

Thus it was that Sor María emerged as a model of holiness as well as innocent of all charges. Apparently the king, Cisneros and the duke of Alba were convinced and managed to convince others that Sor María was not a demonized female but a saint in their midst.

The favorable outcome notwithstanding, Sor María did not enjoy trouble-free years in the order. She seems to have been involved in internal politics for several years after the conclusion of the proceedings. In Rome, Cajetan must have realized that the business of the Beata had its serious side, for on September 15, 1509, and therefore before the fourth examination, he had sent orders that no religious man was to have anything to do with Sor María or any other religious woman of the order, not even to administer the sacraments, without written consent from the provincial. Her confessors lost their license to hear her confessions and the provincial was directed to name new confessors in their place.[18]

Then Cajetan acted to thwart the growing move to secession by the monastery of Piedrahita. Gregorio Pardo and Bartolomé de Torres as principal leaders in Piedrahita were ordered to Rome (October 12, 1509) and four days later Diego de Vitoria was assigned to Córdoba until he was needed at the examination. Diego de Vitoria did not obey the order, even when it was repeated the following February, but then neither had he obeyed a provincial order of June 1509 assigning him to Ávila (December 4, 1509); in 1512 he was still in Piedrahita. Benavente was removed as prior of Piedrahita and Francisco de Porres assigned to Granada by order of February 9, 1510, but by November of 1511 they also remained in Piedrahita. Clearly Cajetan was becoming impatient with the Spanish group, for in the directive of February 9, 1510 he ordered the provincial to determine if the Beata's confessors, including Vitoria, had been in her convent of Aldeanueva; if so, he was to punish them. If the provincial could not punish them, he was to send them to Rome where he, Cajetan, would handle them.

Cajetan's displeasure is unmistakable in his reaction to the sentence rendered by the tribunal: on July 17, 1510 he renewed three orders previously sent to the provincial: one) Sor María was not to leave the convent except to transfer to the house under construction; two) she was not to speak with or write to anyone except her confessor unless she received written permission from the provincial for each and every time; three) her prophecies, raptures and ecstasies were not to be discussed with any people except the provincial, the general or the procurator of the order. Heredia notes that even though the orders were accompanied by the threat of grave punishment, the group at Piedrahita payed no more attention to them than they had the preceding set.[19]

During these years of internal upheaval and until her death around 1524, which is the last year she is mentioned as prioress in the documents of the convent of Aldeanueva, Sor María resided in that house. There is evidence that her old supporters, Diego de Vitoria and Gregorio Pardo, were in Aldeanueva on and off until 1524 and that they had not obeyed Cajetan's directive to halt all communication with the Beata. But by that time tensions within the order had eased and the threat of schism had passed. That Sor María had some part in that dissension is clear, but the details of the story await telling in a later chapter. For now we are left with the impression of a charismatic woman who in her own century was praised and criticized and in our time is regarded by a scholar who displays no more patience than Cajetan with the dissidents of Piedrahita as a singular woman who has left a pleasing, and for some people, an extraordinarily pleasing memory.[20]

Chapter Two

Portrait of a Beata

The gaps in documents that consternate the historian are the stuff of life for the reader with poetic inclination. In the case of Sor María's examination, the records provide testimony from the Beata, her defender and the witnesses, but the specific charges that set in motion the series of investigations are not available in written form. Thus the reader is left to infer the accusations that prompted such lively explanations as to why men spent the night in Sor María's room and sometimes even lay on her bed. Also left to inference are questions about the motivations of her critics and advocates as well as of the woman who was Sor María of Santo Domingo.

1. Rapture

The matter of Sor María's raptures is perplexing because the records not only are inadequate but also contain contradictory testimony.[1] By the Beata's own account she had experienced raptures since childhood in which angels, saints, devils and the Lord himself appeared to her, and the Blessed Mother, the Lord and the saints in heaven conversed with her. She also testified that because she was enraptured when she spoke, she usually could not remember anything she said; she added, however, that Diego de Vitoria was always with her and consequently would know the truth and could say it.[2] In his defense of the Beata, Antonio de la Peña addressed the issue of rapture in fourteen of the forty-four points that constitute the document; from details that he provides it is fair to infer that the Beata was frequently enraptured for long periods of time.[3] There were two aspects to her raptures that were especially remarkable for the witnesses. First, on Thursday evenings and on Fridays until noon or about noon she would represent all the mysteries of the Lord's passion while enraptured (#11). When she came to the moment of Christ's death, it would seem to those present that she also died; she would not come to her senses for a long time and when she did, she was still in a state of rapture (#16). Sometimes when her arms and feet were positioned as if she were on the cross with her right foot on the left one, those present would try to bend her arms out of their extended position and remove one foot from the other, but their efforts were to no avail. She was so firmly positioned as if she were truly on the cross that even their attempts to force her arms and feet free were in vain.

The second noteworthy feature of Sor María's raptures is that she answered questions that learned men who were present would pose about theology, sacred scripture, the sacraments and the afterlife in hell, purgatory and paradise (#12) . Sor María's associates were stunned that an illiterate woman with only a smattering of religious education could answer wisely the subtle questions put to her.

The question that the defense addressed was not if the Beata did what has been described but whether she was inspired by God or was acting on her own. That is, were the raptures genuine or feigned? All fourteen points are wholly or in part statements in defense of the authenticity of the raptures. In two instances the defender concludes the description of the rapture by saying that "It is something marvelous to see" (#11) and that "they [those present] are impressed" (#15). On one occasion the defender is more explicit in his intent to prove the genuineness of the raptures: after reporting that the event seemed miraculous to those in attendance, he draws the intended conclusion for the examiners when he asserts that "there was no way this could be feigned" (#16).

Undoubtedly the charge of pretense had been made, at least in the form of suspicions, and just as surely was Antonio de la Peña resolved to prove that the Beata was anything but a hoax. He made sure that her raptures met two major tests: they came upon her unexpectedly and they bore positive fruit. Not only was the Beata overcome by ecstasy when she prayed, but even while she was eating and out walking in the field or by the river she would suddenly fall into trance (#10). The fruits of her raptures were wondrous to behold: after rapture she always was happy and joyous (#20); if she had been suffering physical pain before the rapture, afterward she felt fine (#21); while she was undergoing the passion in rapture, she was oblivious to any pain except in places of her body where Christ was nailed and bore the crown of thorns—even if others pressed hard on parts of her body that had hurt before, in rapture she was insensible to pain (#21). Her raptures were beneficial to other people as well, for her ecstatic utterances were so inspiring that her listeners wept piously on hearing them (#10).

If further proof was needed that the Beata was not feigning raptures, Antonio de la Peña had at hand four points on her behalf. First, how could a poor, ignorant village woman reply knowledgeably in elegant language and even employ and understand Latin if she was not divinely inspired (#12, #22)? Such was her depth of understanding that she surpassed masters of theology and men of great learning (#12); of course those who heard her were amazed and considered the change in her speech and countenance a marvelous thing (#19), especially when she spoke in the person of Christ or the saints, looking more majestic and beautiful than when she spoke out of trance (#12, #19, #22). The defender's second point was that Sor María was able to read the minds and hearts of those present and far away. Once when a high-ranking prelate sent a person to relay doubts which he had written down, she countered them without even seeing them on the paper or hearing them read (#13). Another time, when she was enacting the passion in her raptured state, she asked a person who was present why he doubted her genuineness; he immediately realized that his doubts were unfounded and in the presence of the others asked her forgiveness as contritely as if he had committed a sin (#14). There were other times, the defender added, when she replied to doubts that the people who harbored them had not even expressed. The third point was that Sor María revealed herself to be a faithful Christian and Catholic, for every word she uttered in rapture was in conformity with the Church's teaching and her prayers were for the welfare of the vicar of the Church, Mother Church, her ministers and Christian princes (#17). Fourth, her Christian compassion and humility were so deep that in ecstasy she tearfully prayed for her persecutors who, she believed, intended her no harm and in truth worked on her behalf because they awakened her to the sinful, ungrateful condition of her soul and consequently helped her to make amends and turn to God with compunction and devotion (#18).

Antonio de la Peña's unshakeable confidence that Sor María's raptures were God-given was not uniformly shared by the witnesses whose testimony is available. Francisco de Porres, however, approaches the defender's enthusiasm when he responds to questions about how she answered theological questions. He affirmed that on one occasion when he heard her speak about sublime theological matters, her listeners were amazed. Among those in attendance was a professor of theology from the university of Valladolid who wept at her marvelous words and confided to this witness that the little woman knew more than all the learned men in the kingdom, for it was the Holy Spirit who had instructed her.[4]

But another witness, Agustín de Funes, had his doubts. Although he had not known her until fifteen days before giving the deposition, he nonetheless believed that her raptures were false on the grounds that she was said to go into trance at will. He was suspicious of her on the two occasions when he had seen her enraptured: the first time she addressed all her words to this witness and the second time she corrected herself when speaking in the person of God and spoke primarily to the judges who were present. To her credit, however, her conversation was edifying, as were the words she uttered in rapture. Even though he had heard many reports of her good life and considered her words good, he nonetheless feared that her raptures were feigned. Juan de Azcona from the monastery of Santa Catalina also testified that her raptures were a hoax.[5]

The witness who was less credulous than others, in the view of Heredia, was Juan Hurtado.[6] Although he was divided in his opinion about the raptures of Sor María, he tended to agree with Agustín de Funes and Juan de Azcona that they were not genuine. Hurtado testified that it was well known that the Beata often conversed with Christ, spoke in his person and in the person of the saints, and uttered secret things while enraptured. He had heard that during her stay in Toledo, where her raptures were a popular topic of conversation, the enraptured Beata had warned the provincial and prior of the monastery to work for religion and reform. Hurtado must have been sincerely troubled by the matter of Sor María, for on the one hand he had heard Cardinal Cisneros say that she was the only living gospel he had seen, while on the other he himself had seen her enraptured so often and seemingly at will during his three years of association with her that he genuinely questioned the authenticity of the ecstasies. It was strange and exquisite, however, that one day in rapture the Beata gave her opinion on a matter that had been troubling his conscience the previous day but which he had not confided to her. Heredia's conclusion about this witness is that although Hurtado did not reject all her raptures, he considered some fake and suspected her of pretense in the case of others.[7] There is also an interesting bit of testimony about the raptures from her confessor; sometimes he had asked Sor María to go into rapture so that certain people could see her and sometimes she would and sometimes she would not.[8]

2. Miraculous Communion, Stigmata, Prophecy

Related to raptures and frequently occurring during them are three extraordinary phenomena: miraculous communion, stigmata and prophecy. With respect to the eucharist, evidence is that receiving holy communion was a spiritually powerful experience for Sor María, who testified that she had seen the Lord in the eucharist and that he had given her a ring, which she kept in her monastery. Her supporters regarded it as a miracle that she was often enraptured at the consecration even though she was not physically present at mass but was in her room (#9). Her advocates also considered miraculous or invisible communion proof of her holiness. Once when a priest went to give the Beata communion and could not find the host that he had consecrated and left on the corporal, he was given to understand by her that she had already received the host (#8). The people like Vitoria who witnessed the phenomenon called it a great miracle and believed that either the Lord or an angel acting on his command had given her communion. Lope de Gaiból, however, had put Sor María and her miraculous communion to the test and in his view she had failed. Once when he had held up an unconsecrated host she had run to the altar in ecstasy as if it were the real thing. For this witness her ecstasies were pure fraud.[9]

Sor María's stigmata was confined to a wound in her right side, which she said had opened for the first time four years previously in Ávila and again later that same year. She added that the duke of Alba had seen the wound as had her confessor, who in turn testified that he, the duke and other religious had seen it. The defense states that on Holy Thursday of 1509 her right side below the ribs opened and blood streamed out (#24). Evidently the examining judges had viewed the side, for the point continues with the statement that she now has the scar of the wound on the same side, as the reverend judges themselves know for they had seen and certified its existence.

Sor María's stigmata seems to have been as well publicized as her revelations. Hurtado had doubts about the authenticity of both, even though one of Sor María's companions and a woman he deemed trustworthy assured him that the wound was not a hoax. Sor Inés adamantly claimed that the wound was genuine and stated that she herself had seen the side open not once but many times.

Father Damian of Ávila testified that once when Sor María was enraptured she clutched in pain at her body where the mark of the wound was and dealt herself blows. Announcing that he could take away the pain with the sign of the cross, Vitoria blessed Sor María and immediately the pain disappeared.

One account by an unidentified witness is dramatic evidence that the stigmata was genuine. As of last lent, the witness said, one year had elapsed since the Holy Thursday when he had given communion to the Beata. Something about her countenance roused his suspicion that her side might not be open. The following day, which was Good Friday, he asked the enraptured woman to petition God's forgiveness for a suspicion that he had, whereupon she replied that the request was unnecessary for what was needed would be revealed. Coming out of rapture about eight or nine o'clock in the morning, she went directly to bed for she was in acute physical pain. Hearing her loud cries of pain, the witness went to her room and at Sor María's request summoned Sor Inés. When Sor Inés entered the room, everyone except the witness went out. When the Beata asked her if anyone was in the room, Sor Inés replied that only the priest remained. For a while Sor María was silent and then, asking if the door was closed and assured it was, she said to Sor Inés: "Sister, put your hand in this side and take out what you find for it causes me grievous pain." Putting in her hand, Sor Inés removed a bloody cloth at which Sor María expressed deep sorrow and was once more enraptured. Then she said to Sor Inés: "Put in your hand more carefully and take out what is hurting me so much." Again her companion put in her hand and took out another small cloth filled with blood. The cloth, Sor Inés said, was in the wound.[10]

The enraptured Sor María often spoke prophetically. (See Chapter Four for her prophecies about reform of the Dominican Order.) "Many times she spoke of what was to come," reads the forty-third point, "and it happened as she foretold." Proof of her prophetic gifts is limited to one example—that before she knew the king or any noble she had prophesied the building of a large monastery in Aldeanueva, which would house many religious women. The point asserts that this prophecy came true as did other unspecified predictions.[11]

The testimony of four witnesses sheds light on the nature of Sor María's prophecies and proves that they not only failed to materialize but were beyond the pale of realistic expectation: that no friar in the monastery of Santo Tomás in Ávila would die during the pestilence; a number of brothers from the house, including Tomás de Mendoza, would soon be martyred, in about a year was the witness's understanding; before she would travel to Rome on the business of reform, another beata by the name of Francisca del Mandato must go, and the two women would meet on the way, enter Rome together and meet the pope; one day 90,000 Moors would be converted; she would go to Jerusalem two times; the king would establish a monastery in Llastas to be inhabited by exceedingly holy men; a very holy pope would come in the person of a man who was alive then but very old.[12]

Some prophecies that have reform for their theme seem to bear out Hurtado's contention that Sor María said things to please her listeners, whose intentions she perceived. Knowing the character of Dominican brothers such as Diego de Vitoria and Francisco de Porres, Hurtado could not believe that they had induced her to say what she did although he did concede that the men were stubborn in their support of the woman. He suspected that there was pretense but it was on her part rather than on theirs.

Surely her Dominican brothers must have been comforted by predictions given in rapture that the Order of St. Jerome was to be changed to that of St. Dominic; Franciscans had to be humbled and not allowed to preach without being examined by the Dominicans; and Dominican friars would join forces with the pontiff to reform the church. They might have been less happy to hear that reform would cost a large number of martyrs from their ranks! Certainly her prophecy that the monastery of Santo Domingo had to be reformed must have put heart into the faction that was agitating for increased austerities in the order.

There is also a bizarre prediction about giving pieces from the heart of her wound to Diego de Vitoria for him to carry as a relic to San Vicente in Ávila.[13]

Juan de Septiembre provides a balanced view of the Beata's prophecies, calling to task people who repeated her predictions over and over. With repetition came excess, as when listeners drew from her prediction on the pestilence the meaning that none of the brethren of Santo Tomás would die, whereas his view was that she had given them no assurance other than hope in the Lord's help. He, Juan de Septiembre, had frequently cautioned others not to speak casually about the affairs of Sor María or to praise her excessively.

3. Dress, Diversions, Food and Fasts, Illnesses, the Devil

Sor María was controversial even in such innocent-sounding matters as what she wore and ate. Her dress must have been the subject of widespread criticism because her defender speaks to it in five points, employing Latin in two of them, a hint perhaps that the charge was indeed grave. Point thirty-two is a description of her clothing and a statement that such dress was not conventional in the order:

> It is indeed no obstacle that some witnesses appear to impute of the said Sor María that about this time she wore or was accustomed to wear curious clothes beyond the propriety of her rule. Specifically a cap on her head, little bracelets on her arms, and a collar and other types of clothes and shoes not according to the convention of her rule.[14]

Three points of defense follow. She did not wear such clothes because she was vain or fickle but to comply with the request of some person. He himself, Antonio de la Peña, who the examiners know to be a religious man and well known in the realm, gave her the little hats and skirts of fine scarlet cloth in order to ease her suffering and because she was a very great handmaid of God (#33). The purse of red satin was also a present, which she used for carrying relics, and the rope of St. Francis she wore at the request of Cardinal Cisneros (a Franciscan) as a means of remembering him in prayer (#33). Nor was she vain about the coral beads and gold and silver ornaments she wore, for sometimes their purpose was to ease pains caused by her heart and then again the ornaments were from people who asked her to wear them for a while and return them to the owners who then treated them like relics (#34). The purity of her intention is all the more evident in the ugly coarse clothing and sackcloth that she often wore as a penitential discipline (#32).[15] Hurtado testified that he had seen or heard from others that she wore fine clothes, gold jewelry and little French hats for her strolls in the countryside. But, he assured the examiners, whenever he saw her and regardless of her attire, she spoke devoutly of holy matters.

Sor María de Cordero, who had known the Beata for four or five years and had lived with her in Ávila, Aldeanueva and Barco de Ávila, attested to Sor María's goodness on all points, including the matter of her dress. Sor María, she said, preferred to wear coarse clothing and put on fine clothes and jewels only in the sense that a religious image or statue might be dressed and decorated. This woman adamantly denied that she had lightened the Beata's hair though she did admit that she had done that for some sisters in the monastery of Santa Catalina.[16]

Obviously Sor María's dress and appearance was a more serious matter than Antonio de la Peña's charming picture of crimson skirts and coral beads and little French hats would suggest. The subject of her attire comes up again in the introduction to *The Book of Prayer* where the editor advances the ingenious argument that her attire is proof of humility rather than pride because wearing colorful clothes and jewelry causes others to think less of her than they would if they did not see this weakness.

Sor María suffered allegations of being a frivolous woman because of her dancing, playing chess and engaging in other diversions as well as her dress and appearance (#35, #36). Perhaps her critics questioned the sincerity of her endeavors to bring about greater austerity in the monasteries when they saw her dance and otherwise divert herself. Her defender maintained that even in the midst of such pastimes her thoughts were always on holy matters; the proof was that when she was thus engaged she would suddenly fall into rapture and speak holy words of unquestionable purity. Hurtado, who had often seen the enraptured Beata dance graciously with Christ and the angels and out of rapture with a relative, offered this curious observation about her amusements: although now, meaning at the time of the examination, the diversions seem frivolous when he hears about them, at the time they were not, and although he does not approve of them, he admits that when he saw her dancing, he and others who were present were moved to tears by the holy things she said. He does not remember seeing her do anything frivolous without there being something holy in it. The testimony is even more intriguing because it comes from the man who doubted the authenticity of her raptures and suspected her of flattering her listeners with prophecies they wanted to hear.

Fasting was a part of Sor María's life of mortification that also won her praise and fame.[17] Even as a small child she underwent severe abstinences and fasts, and after she received the habit of a tertiary she neither ate meat nor drank wine. Much of her life she ate nothing except bread and water and sometimes herbs; in lent and advent she went for days without solid food. After two years without solid food she was unable to keep anything in her stomach; she would vomit so hard that she collapsed from fatigue. Nor did she eliminate "eo modo quo alii homines" (as other people did); the closure of her digestive system was considered miraculous, a divine gift (#5).

Whether her many illnesses were the result of these abstinences or, as some believed, a divine gift, they were so grave that death seemed imminent (#6). A further sign of the miraculous nature of her illnesses and pains was the great patience and charity with which she bore them. She even begged God to send more torment and take from others their pain that she might suffer it for them (#6). Her defender's statements about her health include phrases such as "all who hear of this consider it a marvelous thing," but unanimity on the nature of her illnesses did not prevail. Diego de San

Pedro, who had known the Beata for six or seven years, suspected that she was epileptic or that her extraordinary phenomena were caused by the problems with her heart, which other witnesses had also mentioned. Hurtado concurred that epileptic attacks and cardiac problems accounted for her behavior.[18]

Another possible explanation for her physical suffering was her belief that demons assaulted her day and night with such violence that blood streamed from her mouth, ears and nostrils (#25, #40). Diego de San Pedro testified that in spite of the efforts of four or five men to hold her, the devil still managed to throw her against the wall. Once he found her nearly dead from such an attack, bleeding from her nose, ears and mouth and with a large piece of flesh thrust between her teeth. Sor María confided her fear of the devil to the examiners and described in fascinating detail how the devil had once appeared as half-man and half-horse and another time in a herd of pigs and how he had thrown her down a well where she managed to stay alive by praying the Creed aloud until her sisters heard her and rushed to rescue her.[19]

4. Sexual Conduct

To judge from the defense and the witnesses' depositions, the gravest suspicions about Sor María were about her behavior with men. These are the points in the defense that abound in the use of Latin. The situation appears to be that religious men often gathered in her room to contemplate her ecstasies and listen to her holy words. These men she usually embraced, her face next to theirs, especially when she had not seen them for several days. More serious were the suspicions raised by the knowledge that religious men, and sometimes it was only her confessor, spent the night in her room, ostensibly to protect her against the devil and console her through the intense pain she suffered from her cardiac illness. The situation called for a great deal of explanation; hence the several points in the defense (#36, #37, #38, #39, #40, #41, #42) and the lengthy depositions by the witnesses, as well as the Beata herself, who explained that her confessor would stay with her at night by himself or with others and sometimes he was close to her bed and other times he lay on top of it. He and others spent the night because of her physical afflictions and the devil's attacks. Indeed, Sor María said, Vitoria had once rescued her from the devil himself, who had her upside down and bloodied. Vitoria might have embraced her then and put his face next to hers, but if he had come it was in answer to pleas for help from the other beatas. About embracing, she added that sometimes when she recovered from an attack, Vitoria, Antonio de la Peña and other religious men would hold her close as a way of expressing their joy.

Sor María does not seem to have felt guilty about her behavior. She explained that she was frequently unaware of what she did or said because she was in rapture, and furthermore her confessor ought to answer for her since she always acted in obedience to him. Then there is this wonderfully revealing bit of testimony: "When she implored God to protect her from sins of the flesh, He replied: 'Do not fear daughter, for I will protect you'. Asked if she had ever been tempted by sins of the flesh, she replied that she did not remember having been."[20] Evidently Sor María regarded herself as not only free from sexual temptation and misconduct but divinely protected as well.

The testimony of the witnesses is as compelling as Sor María's. Not unexpectedly her confessor, defender and other avowed supporters swore to the innocence of all parties under suspicion. Diego de Vitoria was the most suspicious of the lot because he had admitted to staying alone with her at night with or without a light and near the bed or on it. It was true, he testified, that he had embraced and kissed the Beata, but never impurely. He thought that those who were present or knew of his actions would have realized that his intentions were absolutely chaste. He did admit under questioning that one or more people had cautioned him to refrain from being with the Beata at night.[21] Although he had complied for a day or two, he resumed communication with Sor María when he saw her need, for he did not believe that he was offending anyone and furthermore his conscience and hers were clear. Finally, he was confident that he was serving the Lord when he stayed with the Beata.

Equally convinced of Sor María's innocence and the pure intentions of men who accompanied her at night was Diego de San Pedro, the prior of the monastery of Santo Domingo of Piedrahita at the time of the examination and destined later to be confessor to Emperor Charles V. He had also spent the night in the Beata's room, at times with as many as four or five others but sometimes in the company of only one person. Questioned about the reason for these overnight stays, he replied that the Beata wanted company, though he was not sure for exactly what reason except perhaps to protect her against the devil's attacks, which she claimed were so violent that not even four or five men could prevent the adversary from hitting her against the wall. Once they found her fallen face down on the crucifix she held in her hands with blood streaming from her ears, mouth and nose and a large piece of flesh between her teeth. Another reason given for staying in her room at night was that men wanted to hear the words she spoke in rapture, which were so holy that they wept with devotion.

At least eight more witnesses, including a female companion to the Beata and a brother of the duke of Alba, corroborated the testimony of these two fervent disciples of Sor María.[22] An unnamed witness reported a conversation that the son of the duke of Alba had told him about: it seems that one had responded to another friar's question about the propriety of Sor María and her confessor being alone at night by asking if Diego de Vitoria and the Beata might not enjoy more grace than St. Peter and Mary Magdalen!

Not all witnesses were as uncritically supportive of the Beata and her confessor as these brothers were. Not surprisingly Juan Hurtado had mixed emotions about the Beata's association with men. Hurtado, it is remembered, had unsuccessfully warned Vitoria against excessive familiarity with Sor María; he had no more success in persuading Francisco de Porres and Tomás de Matienzo to take action against Vitoria. The latter excused himself out of fear of offending the duke of Alba. It was Hurtado's opinion that some of her male supporters would not desist from these familiarities unless they were ordered to do so under threat of excommunication, in which case he was sure they would obey because he knew they were men of good conscience. That remark seems to absolve the men, clearing the way for him to declare that the Beata must have tempted the priest and forced him into suspicious familiarity.

The fullest deposition in the records is from Juan de Septiembre, then prior of the monastery of San Pablo in Valladolid. His testimony reveals a conscientious effort to understand the motives of the parties involved. Having spoken with priests who had known Sor María since childhood and lauded her character and extraordinary gifts, Juan de Septiembre was assured of her virtue as well as the pure intentions of the religious men. Even though the men had done nothing wrong, he believed that they set a bad example by speaking intimately with women. He had reproached those people who spoke too freely about the Beata's affairs or praised her overly much. He was aware of the charges of sexual misconduct because when he was involved as a definitor in the earlier examination in June of the same year, he heard Juan de Medina testify to having seen Vitoria lying on Sor María and having heard Antonio de Benavente admit that Sor María kissed him; she had put her face next to his but he saw nothing unchaste in the act. Septiembre added that in the monastery of San Pablo, where the examination took place, men and women were said to prostrate themselves on her when she was overcome by fainting and heart problems.

When asked why there was such a diversity of opinion about the Beata, Juan de Septiembre responded with remarkable prudence. First, the entire affair exceeded matters of faith which were determined by the Church; hence there was room for speculation about such things as the Beata's revelations. Second—and here he repeated his opinion—there was far too much talk about Sor María; in the constant telling and retelling of her affairs details were added and changed until the accounts seemed hardly possible. The third and for him principal cause for the diversity of opinion and contradictions was that her counsels and prophecies in rapture were not to everyone's liking. The favorable things she said about the Inquisition and her advice to punish *conversos* were exaggerated and recounted to people who took umbrage. Moreover, the reform of the order which the Beata urged while in rapture did not please some members, who resented the imposition of severe disciplines and interpreted the strife that resulted from her efforts at reform as a sure sign that her work did not originate with God. But, the witness countered, her critics were the very people who, even before the Beata pronounced for greater austerity, had not observed the rules of religious life. Furthermore, the same critics had not heard her or spoken with her, nor would they believe people who did know her personally.

In the final analysis, Septiembre was favorable to the Beata, not only because he distrusted the motives of her critics but also for the good fruits of her words and actions. The religious who were able to observe austerity for a while spoke well of her. Also, how could the Lord allow so many devout people, including innocent girls, to be deceived if indeed the Beata's affairs were feigned or the work of the devil. No, he concluded, Sor María's critics were blind to the truth. Beltrán de Heredia, by the way, is convinced by Juan de Septiembre's testimony, discerning in it a basis for truth. Heredia concludes that the examiners must have realized from the testimony that gossip and the imagination worked overtime in her critics.[23]

5. Final Touches and Comments on the Portrait

Juan de Septiembre's testimony on the good fruits of Sor María's life and work is an echo of points twenty-six through twenty-nine of the defense. Her beneficial influence was manifest among religious men and women: the weak in spirit were strengthened by her holy words and virtuous life, and the lukewarm turned fervent in observing disciplines, abstinence and fasts. Her holy life also affected secular men and women: the lapsed returned to the sacraments after many years, the devout became even more devout, and some even entered religious life. And women of all ages and conditions, more than one hundred of them, had left the world to embark on a religious life of exemplary penitence. They neither ate meat nor drank wine unless gravely ill, forsook linen clothing, and received the sacraments more frequently than ordained by their rule. Would the duke of Alba have funded a monastery for them had not Sor María and the women she inspired been for him in turn a profound inspiration? Consider, too, that she was a mother to poor children, doing her best to provide religious education and seeing that they learned their grammar.

A final touch to this portrait of Sor María, which is being drawn on the basis of the documents of her examination, is provided by a short but fascinating piece of testimony from Juan Hurtado. Asked if Sor María heard confessions for some people, he replied that he had heard but did not remember from whom that, yes, she did hear confessions but not "in the sacramental form" and that she had given one or two sermons but not in the manner of preachers. It was impossible for Sor María not to have incurred severe criticism when she came so close to functioning as a priest and stretched to the limit the tolerance of men who considered silence a necessary virtue in women.

Since the understandings about Sor María that develop in reading the defense and depositions of the examination are based on records that are incomplete and undeniably subjective, it is prudent at this point only to highlight the obvious features in the emerging portrait and to withhold a detailed assessment pending additional insights from a study of the currents of reform and dissidence that affected her, as well as from the summary of her life in the introduction to *The Book of Prayer*, which was written after the examination. The Beata was clearly a woman of charismatic appeal for a wide variety of people, and the extraordinary phenomena of rapture, prolonged fasting, opening of her side and miraculous communion were just as clearly a major reason for her appeal. But the phenomena were also the source of criticism. Just as the phenomena cut both ways, now to her credit and now to her discredit, so did tales of lewd conduct with men counter reports of her exemplary life.

Sor María must have believed that she was divinely protected to have endured the storm that enveloped her even though she had the support of Cardinal Cisneros, the king and the duke of Alba and even though the fourth examination was arranged to ensure a favorable outcome. The fact remains that she was an unlettered woman of peasant origins testifying before churchmen of illustrious rank and education. The demands on her physical and spiritual fortitude must have been enormous as she underwent the ordeal. She truly needed to keep faith that God stood with her, and there is every reason to believe from her testimony that she did not fail in the test of faith.

Chapter Three

Reformers, Rebels and Sor María

Whether the date of Sor María's birth is 1470 or 1486, she lived in times of ferment: Spain achieved political unity for the first time in seven centuries and became a citizen of Europe and the world; her arts and education flourished in the invigorating climate of the Renaissance; reform and innovation urged religion to new life. The major step toward political unification of Spain was the marriage of Ferdinand of Aragón (1452–1516) and Isabel of Castile (1451–1504). Called the Catholic Kings by the pope for their unremitting crusade against the Moors that climaxed in 1492 with the capitulation of the kingdom of Granada, Isabel and Ferdinand joined in marriage not only their political estates but also complementary personalities and talents to create a society that nourished cultural accomplishments of the highest order.

The Catholic Kings were politically successful at the expense of the notoriously anarchical nobility; the monarchs curtailed the privileges of the nobles, assumed mastership of the military orders, and secured a uniform judiciary and administrative system. Political unification implied religious and racial unity as well, and in 1478, by authority of a papal bull, the Catholic Kings established the Spanish Inquisition, which was initially commissioned to hear cases of apostasy and subsequently all charges of heresy. After the defeat of Granada, they solidified unity with decrees in 1492 and 1502 that ordered first Jews and later Moslems to convert to Catholicism or leave the country. The cost to Spain for this racial and religious cleansing was untold human suffering and economic catastrophe, as hundreds of thousands of Jews and Moslems elected exile over forced conversion.

Alert to the rebirth of art and learning in Italy, the Catholic Kings persuaded Italian humanists such as Peter Martyr to introduce Renaissance methods of scholarship into Spain and, at the same time, they recalled from Italy their own brilliant scholars for the purpose of enriching Spanish cultural life with the knowledge they had acquired in foreign study. The major figure in the effort to develop Spanish humanism and promote the religious reform that especially preoccupied Isabel was Francisco Ximénez de Cisneros.

1. Cisneros and Religious Reform

During his long life (1435–1517), Cisneros rose to prominence as confessor to Queen Isabel, provincial of the Franciscans in Castile, archbishop of Toledo, primate of the Spains (meaning the New World), inquisitor general as of 1507 and, on two occasions, regent of the kingdom. He dominated the religious scene in the twenty years prior to the outbreak of the Reformation so thoroughly that, in his study on Erasmus and Spain, Marcel Bataillon asserts that "we must turn to him if we want to understand the attitude of Spain with respect to the Protestant reformation."[1]

The fact that Cisneros took seriously his Franciscan vocation is a key to appreciating his attempts at reform. At a time when highly ranked prelates of the Church lived in princely fashion, Cisneros sought to honor the Franciscan vow of poverty even in his capacity as archbishop. His observance of poverty must have been in surprising contrast to the usual habits of archbishops, for the pope wrote a letter in which he urged the Spanish prelate to live in a manner befitting his office.[2]

Religious reform under the leadership of Cisneros proceeded on several fronts. On February 13, 1495 the Catholic Kings acted on papal authorization and commissioned Cisneros to begin reforms in the women's monasteries; shortly thereafter he extended his reforming efforts to all

Franciscan houses. From its beginnings, the Franciscan Order had been divided on the question of poverty, for the conventuals maintained that ownership of property was legal whereas observants decried the practice as being alien to the teachings and spirit of St. Francis. Cisneros acted on behalf of the observants because he respected them as the true followers of their founder; his idea of reform was to take monasteries away from conventuals and install observants in them. The conventuals who resisted the reform found allies among the wealthy nobles, who had funded the houses or converted churches into family pantheons and now did not take kindly to the prospect of losing their income.[3]

The conflict between conventuals and observants was not easily resolved, especially since the conventuals had not only the support of some nobles but also a covey of lawyers in Rome to plead their case. The balance of favor swung now to Cisneros and now against him, until in 1506 and again a few months before his death in 1517, the pope issued Bulls of Concordia by which the two branches retained possession of the houses that were under their respective control at the time.

Cisneros was successful in his work to reform the Franciscan Order as well as the Dominicans, Benedictines and Jeronymites. In his biography of Cisneros, Álvar Gómez de Castro credited the cardinal with realizing a level of monastic life in sixteenth-century Spain that was undoubtedly superior to that elsewhere in Europe.[4]

Sympathetic to the spiritual needs of the general populace, Cisneros turned to the matter of educating the secular clergy and the masses of Christians. The synods of Alcalá and Talavera in 1497–98 addressed the issue of education; one specific constitution required, under threat of fine, that priests teach children Christian doctrine according to a catechism that the cardinal himself had written. His answer to the question of clerical education was to establish the brilliant University of Alcalá de Henares for the explicit purpose of offering a complete curriculum of Church teaching from elementary to higher education. The university had its beginnings as a college which had been founded toward the end of the thirteenth century and which had been incorporated with a Franciscan monastery for half a century before Cisneros placed the corner stone on March 14, 1498 and the university opened its doors to the first students ten years later.

From the beginning, Alcalá was an original among Spanish universities. First, there was no faculty of law since Cisneros regarded litigation with little favor and believed that Spain had more than enough lawyers. Second, the university offered a three-fold approach to theology, with the teaching of Tomism, Scotism and nominalism. The third novelty of Alcalá was emphasis on direct study of the Bible, with the help of the ancient languages of the Old and New Testaments. This return to the sources was echoed in the study of patristic literature.

Recognizing the need for linguistic tools to study the Bible, Cisneros imported scholars to teach Hebrew, Greek, Latin and other Semitic languages. His interest in languages as tools for understanding scripture and his desire to make the Bible accessible to large numbers of people gave rise to the ambitious project of producing the *Biblia Poliglota Complutense,* a Bible in Hebrew, Greek, Aramaic and Latin. The Bible was a collective effort by a team of specialists, hand-picked by Cisneros to work with the best manuscripts available, including several Greek codices that Pope Leo X lent him from the Vatican Library.

The Bible is composed of six volumes; the first contains the Pentateuch; the second, the Book of Joshua up to that of Paralipomenos; the third, the books of Esdras, Tobias, Judith, Esther, Job, Psalms, Proverbs, Ecclesiastes, Song of Songs, Wisdom and Ecclesiasticus; the fourth has the Prophets and the Book of Maccabeans; the fifth, the New Testament; the sixth has an introduction to the Old Testament, a Hebrew-Chaldean dictionary, a list of Hebrew and Greek proper names, a Hebrew grammar and other introductory aids in the work of exegesis. The first volume was printed in January of 1514 and the last appeared on July 10, 1517, just four months before Cisneros died.

The polyglot Bible is justifiably the most famous of Alcalá's accomplishments, but the university also was responsible for the publication of many noteworthy works on theology, liturgy and scripture in addition to grammars, dictionaries and commentaries. Although the humanist basis to the program at Alcalá is unmistakable, Cisneros's primary intention was to provide the finest theological education possible, and all studies had value in that light.

In the climate of open inquiry that Cisneros fostered, a large, diverse number of religious and spiritual works were translated. Writings of Jerome, Augustine and Gregory the Great were made available in Spanish, as well as texts by Aristotle, Cicero, Seneca and Boethius. One of the most popular works that was translated was the *Vita Christi* by Ludolph of Saxony, first edited in Strasbourg and Cologne in 1474 and already accessible in French, Portuguese and Catalan when the Spanish Franciscan, Ambrosio Montesino, rendered it into Spanish in 1501; the work was published in four volumes in the following two years. In the *Vita Christi,* Ludolph had brought together the four gospels into one account of the life of Christ and incorporated commentaries from patristic literature for the purpose of inducing meditation and prayer in the reader. Montesino further contributed to making the New Testament known in Spanish when he revised a Spanish version of the epistles and gospels by arranging them according to the liturgical year and interspersing appropriate sermons among them. These two works were a major source of knowledge about the life and teachings of Jesus Christ for large numbers of Christians who lacked the linguistic skills of a Cisneros.[5]

In his abiding concern for Biblical scholarship, Cisneros could not have failed to know about the humanist scholar Erasmus of Rotterdam. And it is true that Cisneros invited the famous humanist to Spain to participate in the work of the university, but Erasmus declined the invitation, confiding to his friend, Thomas More, that "Spain says nothing to me."[6] The first appearance of Erasmus's name in Spanish documents is in 1516, but the full impact of Erasmianism was not felt in Spain until after Cisneros's death. The

Enchiridion was published in Spain in 1524 or perhaps 1526, at about the same time that Lutheran books made their way into the peninsula.[7]

By all accounts, Cisneros was the foremost voice of his time. Scholar, theologian, reformer, he was in the words of a modern scholar an *"homo complutensis."*[8] A serious, independent thinker devoted to truth and skilled in languages and dialectic, Cisneros gracefully linked three major schools of theology with the Franciscan spirit, classical models and Christian evangelism.[9] Alcalá was Cisneros's dream and its realization, the collective *homo complutensis* which, like its founder, united "the medieval and the modern, Biblical textual criticism and traditional theological schools, Scholasticism and spirituality."[10]

This *homo complutensis* was also the Cisneros who praised the little holy woman of Piedrahita as the only living example of the gospel whom he had known. How this man, who was knowledgeable in the ways of the world and hearts of men, could have been duped by a simple woman is not an easy question to answer, but if on the one hand the cardinal was learned and astute, on the other he was a Franciscan at heart who was searching for God in the purity and simplicity of the devout life. Bound to the ideal of reform, he may have seen in the Beata what he wanted to see—a life lived in quiet, intense devotion to God, a woman persecuted yet persevering out of desire to lead others along a straighter road to perfection. And perhaps she was all he claimed her to be—almost a living saint. There is also another side to the cardinal which may account in part for his attraction to the Beata. Committed to reform and religious purity in the peninsula and the defeat of Moslems elsewhere in the world, he financed a campaign against the Moors in North Africa that saw the capture of Orán, Bugia and Tripoli by 1511. Although Spain was unable to retain control of the African coast by means of its isolated garrisons, Cisneros held fast to his dream of a Christian reconquest of Moslem territory as far as the Holy Land. The cardinal's religious zeal probably opened his sympathies to the ecstatic woman whose excessive piety and disciplines exemplified the austerities she taught.

For the purpose of understanding the Beata as a woman of her times, it is helpful, if not conclusive, to realize that one of her principal benefactors was a man who was largely responsible for the atmosphere of spiritual reform that at once encouraged and set limits on her activities. That she continued to regard him as her protector well after the examination had absolved her of the allegations is clear from letters addressed to the cardinal from her as well as from the sisters at the convent in Barco de Ávila and the brethren at Piedrahita, who persevered on her behalf in defiance of Cajetan's renewed restrictions (July 17, 1510) on communication with her. In April of the following year we hear her ardent, humble words of gratitude to the cardinal:

> Surely, Lord, I believe the Crucified Jesus Christ will purify your heart when He sees how you help and favor those who desire to love and fear God. And because I do not know how to thank you for these favors which you continually do for us and which we hope for, let He who raised you thank you for them, He by whom you do it, by rewarding you with the liberating captivity of His love, and making you a very great warrior in His Church, and defender of the faith and protector of those who seek Him. And because I, Lord, am such an enemy of this life that I do not seem to have been born on this sad island and because in my opinion I am made of its dross, I despair to see the goal so near and our sight so short.
>
> I do not know why your most reverend Worship places under your protection such a little spirit, such a weak and cowardly one who knows how to do battle so poorly and goes out to stand watch so late. I hope in Jesus Christ and in the protection of His cross that with the good accounting I will make about your most reverend Worship, my own, which I consider so bad, will be excused and accepted as good.[11]

References to Sor María appear in letters to the cardinal from her sisters and the religious men at Piedrahita, which treat the struggle within the Dominican Order over the status of the monastery at Piedrahita. The controversy is a key chapter in the story of the Dominican attempts at reform, in which both Sor María and Cardinal Cisneros figure prominently.

2. The Dominicans: Rebellion and Reform

Serious attempts to reform the Dominican Order in Spain in the direction of observance are evident early in the fifteenth century, when a Father Álvaro de Córdoba relinquished his post as confessor to the queen and retired with some religious companions to the monastery of Santo Domingo in Escalaceli near Córdoba to live in conformity with the austere spirit of Dominican life in the thirteenth century. This house and another that was reformed by a companion of his four years later became quiet centers of prayer and study. In 1427 Martin V authorized Córdoba to be prior of Escalaceli and of any other houses in Castile and León that would embrace the observance, and as a result of this papal action later chroniclers considered Córdoba to be the first vicar of the Congregation of the Observance. Records disclose, however, that the house continued under the governance of the province.[12]

Encouragement for the establishment of a Congregation of the Observance came in a letter of 1467, signed by the king and directed to the lords, nobles, authorities, officials and vassals of the kingdom, charging them to respect the work of reforming the Dominican Order, which had the monarch's approval and recommendation. Probably about this time the master general of the order named a vicar over the observants, although it is not until 1472 that Juan de San Martir is identified in that office. The observants were still under the jurisdiction of the provincial in 1474 when the general chapter convened in Rome, where the topic of reform was as much in the air as it was in the Spain of the reforming Catholic Kings. By 1478, major convents in Castile had been incorporated into the reform, and in that same year Sixtus IV issued a papal bull insuring support for the reform in Spain. A story about the monastery of San Esteban in Salamanca illustrates the conflict that beset the reform even in its infancy.

At San Esteban a certain priest, who had papal authorization and the support of the Catholic Kings to proceed with the reform, presented himself one morning in December of 1475 at the doors of the monastery accompanied by the mayor, his soldiers and a letter from the queen to inform the men within that they were to recognize his authority and affiliate with the group of reformed houses. The announcement met with resistance not only from the brethren but also the citizens of Salamanca, many of whom rushed to their aid and forced the reformers to retreat. For ten years the monastery of San Esteban successfully thwarted efforts to bring it into the reform and managed to maintain its competitive edge as a center of theology over the house of San Pablo in Valladolid, which is known as "the cradle of the future Congregation of the Observance in Spain"[13] in recognition of its earlier attempts at reform.

The growth of the Congregation of the Observance was so effective that by 1489 their houses prevailed in the province. A papal bull of 1489 acknowledged their superiority, as Innocent VIII declared among other items that the vicar had the same power over the congregation that the provincial had over the province. The observants also held chapters and issued acts, which are of especial interest in understanding the push for greater austerity that Sor María and her associates advocated in the on-going reform of the sixteenth century.

From the Acts of Seville, 1483: rigor is imposed with respect to enclosure for women and conduct with them; authority to receive women into the third order is reserved to the vicar general; women must be at least forty years old, honest and able to live on their own resources before they may be admitted as tertiaries; no religious men may visit them without permission from the superior for each visit and such permission is not to be granted easily.

From the Acts of Palencia, 1488: monks are forbidden to enter the cells of one another; the dimensions of the habit are strictly regulated; confessors of religious women are advised that except for administering the sacrament of penitence, all correction and punishment of women is to be left to their female superiors.

From the Acts of Salamanca, 1489: the funds of the community are to be kept in a common deposit; there is no dispensation from fasting; linen may be used only in the case of illness; riding on a horse is forbidden, as is the use of shawls while on trips. The Acts of Salamanca mention Piedrahita among the convents that had espoused the reform.

Subsequent chapters instituted ordinances regulating the dress of tertiaries and proper conduct with them, the admission and term of residence for secular people in convents, and the use of quilts, limiting them to the infirmary and hospice. By this time names that are familiar in the story of Sor María appear in the records—Francisco de Porres, Diego Magdaleno and Juan Hurtado.

The *de facto* union of the province and Congregation of the Observance occurred when Diego Magdaleno was named vicar general of both the congregation and province (1499–1501). Although Magdaleno encouraged the official union of the two branches at the chapter held in Toledo in February of 1500, efforts failed because electors from unreformed houses did not attend. The same meeting saw Antonio de la Peña from the house of Piedrahita elected provincial, but the election was declared void for failure to observe constitutional procedures. However, a year and a half later the master general of the order, Bandelli, confirmed the election of Antonio de la Peña vicar of the reformed houses, a post which he held until 1503 when he went to serve at court at the behest of Queen Isabel. Although the Catholic Kings, the duke of Alba and Cardinal Cisneros supported Antonio de la Peña, he fared less well with the chroniclers of the order, who criticized him for his fanatical approach to reform and support of the Beata.[14] His fanaticism must have been known because when Bandelli issued ordinances to the Chapter of Peñafiel, he revoked the excessive practices of the past and thus tacitly disapproved of Antonio de la Peña's severe program of reform.

From 1508 to 1511 the Dominican scene was stormy even though the union of the two branches had been formalized since September of 1506. For reasons clear only to King Ferdinand, Cisneros and himself, Thomas Cajetan, who had been elected master general in 1508, was not favorably disposed to Magdaleno, whom the previous master general had charged with the thorny task of uniting the Spanish Dominicans. That the affairs of the order were anything but settled during these years is apparent in the succession of six provincials in three years and the fact that Magdaleno feared his adversaries in the order so much that he requested and was granted from the king a safe conduct through the kingdom.[15]

For at least one modern historian of the Dominican Order as well as chroniclers closer to the events, the root of the difficulties was deep in the soil of the house of Santo Domingo in Piedrahita that served as the center of the rigorous reform inspired by Sor María and her colleagues. These were years when Sor María was under investigation and the order was sharply divided in its opinion about the authenticity of her raptures and the propriety of conduct between the Beata and certain male friends. Cajetan acted resolutely to quell the controversy and return the Beata to less conspicuous and, he hoped, less scandalous behavior. In a letter of June 29, 1508 Cajetan wrote to the province exhorting the members of both sides to make peace and submit to the legitimate superior. He also reproved novelties and spoke in an unmistakably sharp tone about the Beata:

> I prohibit you from allowing Sor María of Santo Domingo to enter your convents wherein conduct with women ought to be avoided, and for them [women] to presume to intervene in matters of reform, which are things that concern prelates and not women, whose head is man. I would not want Satan to try to introduce himself through deception into this in order to derive some benefit therefrom. The things that seem supernatural in that good woman are not so clear up to now that on their account we are going to prescind from the norms that religious tradition has approved and our forefathers have always observed. Christ Himself did not entrust the governance of the Church to his most chaste Mother but rather to St. Peter, the fisherman, and his successors, leaving his Mother entrusted to his beloved disciple.[16]

Even after the examination of Sor María resulted in a favorable judgment, dissension in the Dominican ranks did not subside immediately. In her letter to the cardinal, cited above, Sor María thanks him for his continuing support, apparently for the reform she sponsored as opposed to the moderate changes advocated by the majority in the order. The seriousness of the division over reform was such that the house of Piedrahita wanted to secede and form an autonomous congregation. In his history of the Dominican Order, written around the middle of the century, Juan de la Cruz stated that the convent of Piedrahita, in its desire for stricter observance, wanted to separate from the province. "For reasons of increased austerity," he explained, "and also because of growing self-interest, the dissidents wanted to be exempt from obedience to the Provincial who at that time was Diego Magdaleno, whom we mentioned above, and form a particular congregation in the Province whose head would be the convent of Piedrahita where those fathers were gathered, assisted by the great authority and reputation for sanctity which the beata of the order, called María of Santo Domingo, enjoyed in the Province and all the Kingdom."[17]

There are also two documents in the national archives which summarize petitions to exempt the convents of Piedrahita and Aldeanueva from the order. The document concerning Aldeanueva carries an introductory note in Spanish to the effect that the king supports the petition while both documents mention the archbishop of Toledo (Cisneros) and the bishops of Ávila and Salamanca as also supportive.[18] Since Magdaleno was relieved of his duties in the summer of 1508, there must have been evidence of some desire or effort to break away from the province prior to the fourth examination of the Beata late in 1509.

Letters addressed to Cardinal Cisneros from Diego de Vitoria, Sor María, the priests of Piedrahita and the nuns at Barco de Ávila on the one side and officials in the order who opposed secession on the other reveal that the controversy wore on for almost three years after Sor María was cleared of charges and, by order of Cajetan, directed to remain in her convent and male religious forbidden contact with her except by written permission of the provincial. The letters underscore the seriousness of the situation and the pivotal role that Cisneros played in the drama. On May 30, 1510 Vitoria writes the cardinal: "We dare not beseech you not to cease caring for our affairs and needs, for we know that you know better than we what is right for us therein, and we are certain that you will remember them just as you do us."[19]

The letter from Sor María thanking the Cardinal for his support (cited above) is from the following year, April 1511. Late the same year several men from Piedrahita, including Diego de Vitoria and Diego de San Pedro, petitioned the cardinal's help on behalf of their mother, their holy company [of nuns] and themselves. Although "the nature of the adversary and the world are to be feared," they trust that in His infinite goodness the Lord will hear them, and as to the most reverend cardinal, they will say no more, for with him they are to consider "the works of prayer and service" rather than words. They conclude the letter by stating that they will write more later, after they receive a reply from their mother "who with her illnesses has not been able to write more quickly to his most reverend Worship."[20]

On December 31, 1511 Gregorio Pardo writes fervently to the cardinal that he is remembered continually in both Piedrahita and Aldeanueva for he is their "only father, lord and support on earth." They sing litanies for the unity of the Church: the day when the nuns in Aldeanueva learned there was an anti-pope, their mother assembled all her daughters and they sought to break open the heavens with their most sorrowful lament, "calling upon their Spouse to look after His Church, and they walked in processions with their litanies, some of them singing, some crying".[21]

Cardinal Cisneros's fidelity to the Beata and the reformers is unmistakable in Diego de Vitoria's letter of March 1512 from Aldeanueva in which he writes that he stays on in the Beata's convent in order to administer communion to her each day and to carry out the cardinal's instructions that he "write down her contemplations."[22] From September of the same year comes another letter signed by several of the fathers at Piedrahita, a passionate appeal for help on the occasion of their being summoned to Rome, a hint that Cajetan was not pleased with the activities of the brethren of Piedrahita, who must have continued their rebellious ways in spite of a move by the then provincial, Loaisa (elected the end of October or beginning of November 1511), to settle the affair. Loaisa had requested and received (April 24, 1512) authorization to dispense the dissidents from punishment incurred by their disobedience if they would act with reason.

The summons was a signal for renewed appeal to the cardinal in September:

> . . . with humble reverence kissing your sacred hands, we advise you that a few days ago they presented us here a summons to Rome, sent on the request of the procurator of the Order and the Provincial, naming certain people in particular, which matter the venerable fathers Fray Diego de Vitoria and Fray Bartolomé de Torres will relate to your most reverend Worship at greater length and whom we beseech you to believe completely. Because your reverend Worship knows that we poor little ones have no one to protect and defend them in the land of the ministers of their God except your most reverend Worship, may you, Lord, out of reverence for that celestial Father, desire to look with eyes of pity and order the defense and protection of this little flock that desires to desire completely to give itself to the service of the One Who created and redeemed them. See, Lord, your most reverend Worship, how furiously and cunningly they want to undo this holy union. So may you protect us as lord and defend us as our guide and governor. And we go on beseeching the King of kings to make you a column in the Church triumphant as He did in the Church militant.[23]

The nuns at Barco de Ávila added their voices in an eloquent defense of their life and appeal for protection:

> Our precious mother directs us to write to your most reverend Worship so you may know that you have here,

> poor women, unworthy to be called daughters of such a loving father as your most reverend Worship is, more than one hundred and sixty religious, and about thirty secular women who serve, all of us, though sinners, as very great, continual chaplains of your most reverend Worship; and, also to let your most reverend Worship know our fear that this father of ours, the master Fray Diego de Vitoria, wants to leave us, and we truly receive very great suffering from this with respect to our consciences, for we realize that he has always been our father and that God gave him to us as such. By the love of the most glorious Resurrection of all our good, Jesus Christ, we beseech your most reverend Worship to order this disconsolation not to befall us, which is something you can do.[24]

Cisneros was receiving letters from the opposition as well as pleas for help from Sor María and her companions. The provincial, Alonso de Loaisa, writes on October 12, 1512 that the split in the order is a dangerous poison. He appeals to the cardinal to besiege the door to such great evil for "in the hand of your most illustrious Worship" is the power to prevent disunity. "In the rectitude, constancy and word of your Worship," the provincial continues, "I am confident that there never will be division in your time."[25] Four days later he reiterates the plea that the cardinal intervene: "I desire this agreement," he writes, "for the service of God and good of our religion," and he adds that there were truly many priests at Piedrahita "for whom I have special affection."[26] Another four days and a letter signed by Loaisa and thirteen associates implores Cisneros not to aid the priests of Piedrahita in their effort to break away, for such an act will not benefit them and will damage the province, and to make the dissidents obey. The signers promise in the name of the entire province that the provincial will honor conditions which are acceptable to the dissidents; that is, they are not to be moved from Piedrahita against their will and they are to be allowed to live as austerely as they wish.[27]

The provincial writes on November 1, 1512 asking the cardinal to assure Francisco de Porres of the community at Piedrahita that the province sincerely intends to keep the promise about treatment of the brothers there. Loaisa asks help from the cardinal so that "all may be one and we may be at peace."[28]

Schism finally was averted thanks in large part to the tact of the provincial, Alonso de Loaisa, and the efforts of Cajetan. Beltrán de Heredia, whose scholarship on the history of the Dominican Order is invaluable, believes that the dissidents slowed down the work of reform by fifteen years and he blames Cisneros for having thwarted true reform.[29]

The stricter reform that Sor María and the houses at Aldeanueva and Piedrahita advocated had precedent in fourteenth-century Italy with the example of Catherine of Siena and in the following century in the work of Girolamo Savonarola (1452–1498), the preacher and prophet from Ferrara whose sermons and visions made him a popular champion of spiritual and political reform. Although Savonarola's radical actions eventually led to public execution in 1498, his reputation as a religious reformer survived and profoundly influenced the Spanish Dominicans.

One link between Spanish and Italian Dominicans is documented in the 1460s when Spanish Dominicans commonly emigrated to Italy in order to follow the austere regimen of the houses of the Congregation of Lombardy. As the Spanish communities of observants increased in number and membership diminished in the houses of the conventuals that the observants took over, word went out to the Spanish Dominicans living in Italy that they should return to help fill up the houses now under the jurisdiction of the observance. Another link is seen in documents of 1504, which authorized a change in the procedure for naming definitors that would bring the Spanish province into accord with the Congregation of Lombardy.

The congregation in Italy that influenced the Spanish reformers most was that of St. Mark in Florence where Savonarola instituted major reforms after his election as prior. The Spanish reformers emulated the practices of St. Mark in terms of rigorous austerities, the short, narrow habit, mystical dances, the style of singing, love of processions and enthusiasm for prophecies and revelations.[30]

That Savonarola was a visionary given to prophecy and revelation is no small detail in establishing a connection between his reform and that of the Dominicans centered at Piedrahita and grouped around their own visionary, Sor María of Santo Domingo. Traditionally the Dominican Order had emphasized not revelation but reason, not prayer but study, although the case of Catherine of Siena gives lie to the belief that supernatural phenomena and contemplative prayer had little place in Dominican life. Nonetheless, the public and excessive display of rapture by Sor María was not palatable to the majority of her Dominican brothers, many of whom were acquainted with Vincent Ferrer's injunctions against raptures in his *Treatise of the Spiritual Life,* which was translated into Spanish and published in 1510. It is also true, however, that the 1510 edition did not include chapters eleven and twelve that denounce raptures *(arrobamientos)* as madness *(rabiamienta),*[31] an excision which is accountable by the fact that raptures were more acceptable to the Franciscan Cisneros, who had ordered the translation, than to the Dominicans.[32]

But if the Dominican reformers sought authorization for increased austerity on the basis of Savonarola's ecstatic precedent, the Beata was conveniently in their midst; she was a woman who by many accounts was genuinely pious and arguably bore a startling resemblance to Catherine of Siena and Angela of Foligno, both of whom suffered in their bodies the miraculous wounds of Christ, abstained from food for extremely long periods and received visions and revelations.

Although Sor María herself could not have read the writings of the two Italian women visionaries, it is not far-fetched to suppose that she knew about them through her friend, Antonio de la Peña, who had translated the life of Catherine at the order of Cisneros. The first edition was printed by Brocar on March 27, 1511 and the second appeared on June 26, 1511. The translation of Catherine's letters and prayer was also ordered by Cisneros and it, too, is said to be the work of Antonio de la Peña; it was published on November 22, 1512.[33] The writings of Angela of Foligno had appeared in Spain as early as 1505.[34]

The claim that Cisneros and the Beata's supporters wanted a Catherine of their own to legitimate their version of reform through her visions and revelations has some convincing evidence on its behalf: the prominent and favorable position of Catherine in Dominican tradition; the on-going association of Italian and Spanish Dominicans in the formative years of the reform, from around 1475 to 1515; and the circulation of the writings of the Italian saint in Spanish. The Beata need not have read Catherine's writings to know about her, as well as Angela of Foligno, from the likes of her confessor, Vitoria, and the translator, Antonio de la Peña.

One insistent question is whether the Beata was a pawn in the hands of the reformers at Piedrahita, a willing participant, or—and this scenario seems improbable—a schemer bent on exploiting Cardinal Cisneros, King Ferdinand and all her admirers for personal gain. Given the still limited documentation, a prudent answer is that the Beata happened to be among reform-minded people who believed that she was genuinely holy and who had faith that the Holy Spirit empowered both laity and religious and both women and men. The furor over the Beata probably erupted from a failure of circumspection by those who witnessed or heard about her behavior and exaggerated their own accounts for better or for worse. Certainly there are hints in the records of the examination that gossip and excessive credulity played a part in making the Beata a cause célèbre.

With respect to the possibility that Sor María was a schemer, there is no evidence that she aspired to power. The most severe criticism that modern scholars level against her is that she was overly zealous, gullible and neurotic. Even Beltrán de Heredia, who is certainly no fan of hers, claims no more against Sor María than indiscretion and psychotic behavior.[35]

The fact remains, however, that Sor María was a visionary woman among Dominican reformers, and if she did not exactly parallel the famous saint of Siena, she was remarkably similar to her Italian contemporary, Sor Lucia of Narni, who died in 1544 and was beatified by Clement XI.

Sor Lucia enjoyed the support of the wealthy duke of Ferrara, who in 1501 financed the foundation of a magnificent monastery for her which housed more than seventy women within two years. Sor Lucia was esteemed not only in Italy but also in Spain for her virtue, raptures and stigmata; even Alexander VI wanted to see and speak with the holy woman. Her popularity in Spain is evident in this notice from an inventory of papers in the archives of the monastery of San Pablo in Burgos:

> A letter from Hercules, Duke of Ferrara, authorized, in which he says how in the city of Ferrara there was a religious woman of the Third Order of Saint Dominic called Sor Lucia of Narni, a person of very holy and chaste life, who actually had the wounds and stigmata of Christ on her body.

The date is October 27, 1501. Shortly thereafter the letter circulated throughout Spain in printed form.[36]

The Chronicle of Olmeda shows that the remarkable similarity between Sor Lucia with her wealthy duke of Ferrara and Sor María with her duke of Alba did not go unnoticed in Spain at that time:

> Lest we fail to speak of things commonly discussed, there is in our own Spain these days a certain sister of the order of penitence who is popularly called the beata and who, when she is seen undergoing raptures of this kind and ecstasy beyond measure, supplied kindling for no little hatred, dissension, envy and scandal, even among foreigners, with certain people saying that she is good and others saying that she is not good but rather is satan's angel transformed into an angel of light. Indeed, with the king looking after it and with the Lord ordaining, no disgrace is imputed to the Order nor is anything done by that sister which is deemed worthy of death. She was finally sent back in peace to her own convent of Aldeanueva which she had built there, a magnificent place and the site of these happenings. There is another sister in Italy named Lucia of Narni who not only is enraptured

> up to heaven like ours and like the one called the Syracusan, but it is said that she also is marked with Christ's stigmata so that with the authority of the prelates the image depicted and the marks of his wounds go forth into the marketplace. After many prayers to God these marks came to an end and vanished as if they had never been.[37]

In rapture Sor María also mentioned the name of Savonarola. The Beata herself testified that once when she received communion she saw the Lord and a friar who identified himself as Girolamo of Ferrara and held a lily and palm in his hand. She told Vitoria about the vision after she came out of rapture and said that Savonarola's glory was so great that he ought to be canonized. Her confessor later denied hearing her say anything about canonization; neither did Diego de San Pedro remember if she had spoken of canonization with respect to Savonarola or Sor Lucia, although he had heard her say in rapture that Girolamo was glorified in heaven. An unidentified witness affirmed that he had heard her say both in and out of rapture that Savonarola was unjustly executed and that the pope (whom she did not specify) would soon reveal Savonarola's innocence with much honor and glory. The business of canonization evidently caused quite a stir, for Damian of Ávila, Juan Hurtado and Antonio de Benavente testified that they had heard the Beata foretell such an event either directly or indirectly.

Marcel Bataillon maintains that the fact of Savonarola's execution had not diminished but rather enhanced the monk's reputation for saintliness in Spain. When Savonarola's little book on the psalm "Miserere mei Deus" was published in Spain in 1511 at the initiation of Cisneros, it found an eager audience. In an effort to establish a connection between Savonarola and Sor Lucia in Italy and Sor María and her supporters in Spain, it is also worth noting that Antonio de la Peña favored Savonarolaism from the beginning and that he was a major force in promoting translations that the group at Piedrahita made and offered to Cisneros for publication.[38]

The evidence is convincing that the Spanish reformers regarded Sor María as their private oracle and that she herself claimed the role as hers. The third selection of her contemplations in *The Book of Prayer* exemplifies her oracular function. In answer to questions about progress toward Christianization of the New World, Sor María replies in the person of the Lord that successful evangelization depends on the spiritual state of the missionaries:

> "If the fire is not lit or if it drifts to places where it is quickly extinguished, how can the rotten wood be lit that is mired in the slime of sin? First the fire must be lit where there is greater means and capacity for it so that where there is not such great means and capacity it may last and not die out so quickly. Therefore, when the marvelous flame of My love begins to shine in despoiled Spain, many other men of Mine will go forth who will not act like those who are there now. For these will act like brothers to those who are in that land, weeping, eating, speaking with them and describing such things as the heavenly city. And with the love they will show them and the beauty which they will see described, these men will win souls and bring them to Me." (178)

Sor María's plea for inner reform comes at the end of a series of questions that resound with the grave moral and theological debates of her day. The discovery of the New World brought the Spaniards into contact with such radically different cultures that their understandings of what constituted humanity were sorely tested. Even the most compassionate and tolerant of the missionaries that accompanied the explorers must have been appalled at the spectacle of human sacrifice and wondered if the Indians were truly human. Some Spaniards took the position that the Indians were nothing more than beasts and thus deserving of harsh treatment while others pleaded tolerance for the peoples of the New World. By 1510 in the first Spanish settlement of Santo Domingo (1494) the friar Antonio de Montesinos had already begun preaching a moral campaign on behalf of the Indians which Bartolomé de las Casas and other humanitarian Spaniards would join.

The underlying question that stirred debate about treatment of the Indians was whether they were human. If the Indian was human, then he shared with the Spaniard the journey to salvation for which all mankind was destined. Acknowledging the Indian's humanity meant that he participated in the Good News that God revealed to all his creation. So said the Lord through Sor María in response to the first question posed to the ecstatic Beata. Dominicans and later on a good number of Jesuits agreed with the concept of innate grace but the Franciscans were less sure. Having seen barbaric religious practices in the New World, the Franciscans were inclined to believe that the Indians were utterly ignorant of God and therefore in dire need of evangelization, preferably by them.

The issue of evangelization was in the air as well as on Sor María's oracular lips. Had the Indians been evangelized previously and if so, by whom? Sor María's reference to an originally virtuous people in the New World who later were blinded by wicked men coming from Egypt suggests that she subscribed to the theory that the world was evangelized shortly after the Lord's resurrection. The statement by the evangelist Matthew that "This Good News of the kingdom will be proclaimed to the whole world as a witness to all the nations" (24:14) was interpreted to mean that evangelization spread rapidly throughout all the world with the first apostles. The likely candidate for the job of evangelizing was the apostle Thomas who, according to tradition dating back several centuries, had carried his missionary labors to India. For the early Spanish explorers, whose limited geography had them joining eastern India with the western Indies, the possibility of St. Thomas having preached among the Indians was not strained.[39] Sor María's words about evangelization of the New World were especially timely since many Italian and Spanish Dominicans emigrated to the New World between 1507 and 1515.[40]

As the oracle for reform within the order, Sor María found herself at the center of a storm that threatened the existence of the Dominican Order in Spain for several years before and after the turn of the century. With faithful allies in the order she may have edged close to rebellion, but when she is compared to a group of men and women who incurred not merely ecclesiastical suspicion but condemnation by the Inquisition, it is clear that Sor María did not slip over the edge into heresy.

Chapter Four

Heresy: A Case of Mistaken Identity

Although Sor María and Cardinal Cisneros were worlds apart in background, status and learning, they shared the inner world of Christian piety and an ardent desire to purify religious practice through monastic reform. The yearning for deeper, individual spirituality went far beyond the cloister, however, as large numbers of laity and religious responded to a general invitation to interiorize their Christianity. An outpouring of ascetical-mystical literature, bold experimentation in prayer, and the emergence of lay men and women as guides along the inner way are the hallmarks of a spirituality that sought to rekindle the simple piety of primitive Christianity.

The flowering of a personal devotion that probed the spirit beneath the letter of ecclesiastical rules and the sacraments was seeded in the *devotio moderna* that went back at least two centuries in Europe and in Spain yielded its most abundant harvest in the sixteenth century. If the maturation of the fruit had to await the care of a John of the Cross and Teresa of Ávila in the second half of the century, the spiritual labor of visionaries, mystics and theologians in the years up to about 1535 was its necessary preparation and significant as well in its own right. Among other tasks, the spiritual writers of the earlier generation shaped and resolved problems that cleared the way for the comprehensive texts of the later mystics.

The literature of the early period reflects the growing concern for the spiritual life of the individual. Not only were the writings of Bonaventure, Anselm, John Climacus,

Agustine, Jerome, Catherine of Siena and Angela of Foligno translated into the venacular but original works issued from the pens of Spanish writers. Among the earliest and most important of the century were the *Chariot of Two Lives* by García Gómez and the *Exercises of the Spiritual Life* by García de Cisneros; both were published in 1500. A cousin of Cardinal Cisneros, the Benedictine García de Cisneros structured his treatise according to both the traditional ways of purgation, illumination and union and the seven days of the week, thus providing a systematization of the inner journey that would appeal to secular and religious people alike.[1] Two other noteworthy works in the development of spiritual literature were *The Art of Serving God* (1521) by the Franciscan Alonso de Madrid and the *Spiritual Exercises* (1522) of Ignatius of Loyola, the first a methodical presentation of mystical theology and the second a set of rigorous exercises meant to be practiced with the guidance of a director in the context of a retreat.

The literature of the period reflects the growing belief that prayer is essential for the moral and spiritual perfection of the individual. As men and women shunned rote recitation of formulaic words, they turned inward to reflect on sacred scripture and create their own praying in the heart. The term given to prayer wherein the individual relies on her own words and thoughts is "mental prayer." The point of mental prayer is to form an individual mode of communication with God on the personal journey of relationship with the Divine. The movement is thus from external to internal, complex to simple, and rote to spontaneous.

But the matter of prayer was not simply encouraging people to interiorize; questions arose about how to interiorize. Some people advocated consciously centering physical, emotional and mental energies in order to think quietly about God; for them there was work to do. Others taught that prayer was abandonment to God; for them the only work was "letting go." The former called their mental prayer *recogimiento,* or recollection, while the latter spoke of *dejamiento,* or abandonment.

A follower of recollection, Francisco de Osuna wrote the *Third Spiritual Alphabet* (1527) to clarify the nature, modes and desirability of this form of mental prayer. He described the inner life through increasingly subtle experiences of recollection, from the initial action of consciously recollecting the senses, emotions and faculties to the most delicate inward awareness of being recollected in the divine embrace. Osuna is orthodox in his treatment of an inner journey that engages the soul in the active search for God while at the same time recognizing divine grace as essential to spiritual perfection. For Osuna the soul is both active and passive in its journey along the conventional ways of purgation and illumination into union.

Although Osuna's work was published after the probable date of Sor María's death (1524), the *Third Spiritual Alphabet* responds to questions about prayer that were argued in her lifetime and became crucial in the matter of determining religious orthodoxy. Prayer, for example, was a major consideration in the proceedings whereby the Inquisition judged whether individuals were heretical in the manner of the *alumbrados*. The issue of heresy in the case of the *alumbrados* is of consequence in this study of Sor María for the reason that her name has long been linked with the heretics and a great deal of writing has gone into the effort to prove that she either was, or was not, an *alumbrada* and therefore guilty of heresy.[2]

Osuna's importance lies also in the legacy to later mystics that his writings in the *Third Spiritual Alphabet* and other works offered in terms of prayer and inner experience.[3] His clarification of recollection in orthodox terms provided a necessary distinction between active prayer and passive prayer for Teresa of Ávila, who admitted in her spiritual autobiography that Osuna's *Third Spiritual Alphabet* was the first book on prayer she had read. With his clarifications in mind she did not run the risk of the *dejados* (followers of *dejamiento*) who were under suspicion for denying to the soul the need to act on its own behalf.

The practice of mental prayer developed both in and out of the monasteries. The houses where it flourished were predominantly Franciscan; some monasteries such as Escalona were associated with the *recogidos* who practiced *recogimiento* while others, notably Guadalajara, were centers for the *dejados.* But mental prayer was not exclusive to monks; a striking phenomenon of the period is the emergence of charismatic spiritual leaders among the laity, including a surprisingly large number of women. Not only did lay men and women attract followers from the laity but among their students and disciples were priests who, like the preacher Francisco Ortiz and Francisco de Osuna, were prominent leaders in the Franciscan family. The situation appears to be a kind of "democratization" of spirituality with lay and religious alike gathering in small groups for prayer and the interpretation of scripture. Critics called the groups "conventículos" or little convents.

Dejamiento was the form of mental prayer that the *alumbrados* were said to practice. Their practice of *dejamiento* along with their attitude toward the authority of the Church caused the Inquisition to pronounce their teachings and practices heretical in the Edict of Toledo, 1525, and to single out men and women for examination and in several cases for condemnation.

As the past particle of the verb *alumbrar,* which means to enlighten, the word *alumbrado* was a conventional metaphor for divine enlightenment long before its association with the *dejados* in the environs of Madrid, Guadalajara and Toledo in the decade of the 1520s. Originally positive in meaning, the term took on a negative connotation when it was applied strictly to these people.

The doctrinal origins of the *alumbrados* have been the topic of extensive research. Miguel Asín Palacios proposed an Islamic origin, but a more recent scholar of *iluminismo* (from the verb *iluminar* which means to illumine and to enlighten) discounts that theory as well as the idea advanced by Menéndez Pelayo and seconded by Pierre Groult that the movement had its source in German mysticism or that it owed something to Italian mysticism. Other theories about the origins of *iluminismo* have stressed elements of Judaism, Erasmianism, Lutheranism and Anabaptism, while some claim antecedents in medieval Christian heresies. Américo Castro explained its birth in the unrest of large numbers of people who had been disenfranchised religiously when Jews and Moslems were ordered to convert to Christianity or leave their homeland. Studies of individual men and women who were denounced as *alumbrados* support his theory in that *conversos* were prominent in their ranks.[4] Such theories are fraught with contradiction; for example, *iluminismo* was an autonomous movement unrelated to any group or idea outside of Spain,[5] but at the same time it represented "a new step of evolution within European Christian heterodoxy" whose "tradition is as assured as its novelty and originality."[6]

It seems that a combination of spiritual movements outside of Spain, the long, rich tradition of European mystical-ascetical writing that was transmitted to Spain in translation, and original writings in Spanish urged to fruition the evident desire to nurture an inner life of prayer that, for the most part, was an integral part of Catholic practice. The *alumbrados* arrived on the Spanish scene "against the background of a general European religious revival of profound spirituality and mysticism, fostered in Spain by the Cisnerian reform and Franciscan enthusiasm."[7]

Iluminismo asserted itself at three different times in three locales: first in the kingdom of Toledo from 1519–1529, second in Extremadura from 1570–1579, and finally in Andalusia, 1575–1623. Not only were major points of belief and practice set in the first group centered in Toledo, but the function and importance of women was also an established precedent. For the purpose of understanding the frequently alleged connection of Sor María and the *alumbrados,* the following description of the heresy in the kingdom of Toledo focuses on three women.

Francisca Hernández was born near Salamanca, not far from where Sor María spent her life. In fact, she was a contemporary of the Beata as there is evidence that around 1515 she was preaching in Salamanca to friars, clerics and lay folk. Francisca attracted devoted male disciples, among them Antonio Medrano, who moved around with her and was known to remain at night in her house, and Francisco Ortiz, who sacrificed his own career to defend her against charges of heresy. Reports of scandalous behavior with men and suspicious religious practices led to investigation by the Inquisition in 1519, with the result that she and Medrano were ordered to live at least five leagues apart, a directive they defied. As Francisca's behavior continued to rouse suspicions, she was brought again before the Inquisition toward the end of 1530 and this time she confessed at least indirectly to unchaste actions.[8]

The second charismatic woman among the *alumbrados* was Isabel de la Cruz, born in Guadalajara and by profession a seamstress who taught embroidery to girls of the nobility. A third order Franciscan, she was already a spiritual leader by 1512 with disciples from the ranks of both laity and religious in Guadalajara. Her teaching of *dejamiento* was one factor that brought her to the attention of the Inquisition; around 1519 a secret trial began and in 1524 she was investigated officially. The trial ended five years later and she was sentenced to appear in an *auto da fe.*[9]

Isabel de la Cruz influenced another Franciscan tertiary by the name of María de Cazalla whose activities were in Pastraña, where she held religious meetings, preaching, interpreting sacred scripture and teaching *dejamiento*. She was first denounced to the Inquisition in 1525 but not held for extensive questioning until 1530, when a new trial against her commenced. After two years in prison, during which time she defended herself against all charges and firmly insisted on her innocence, even under torture, she received a light sentence; obliged to abjure, though not in public, she was to stand before the sanctuary of her parish church holding a lighted candle and pay one-hundred gold ducats for the expenses of the trial. María de Cazalla is considered to be one of the most spiritually refined and prudent of the *alumbrados* and a woman of integrity and fortitude.[10]

The prominence of women among the *alumbrados* and evidence that their early activities approximate in time those of Sor María indicate why the Beata has traditionally been affiliated with the heretical movement. But a comparison of her teachings, based on selections from *The Book of Prayer,* with the Edict of Toledo shows that the grounds for that connection are anything but firm.

The edict of September 23, 1525 is a document of forty-eight propositions based on statements which the accused and witnesses gave during the proceedings of the Inquisition. The principal doctrinal error that informs many of the propositions is the belief that intimate relationship with God could be realized without any intermediary whatsoever. Not only was the Church, with its sacraments, priests, rituals and emphasis on works, unnecessary but strict adherence to its regulations hindered the soul's journey to God. The *alumbrados* also denied the efficacy of vocal prayer and meditation on Christ's humanity, the existence of hell, the divine origin of confession, the legitimacy of vows, the validity of religious orders, and the authority of the saints' teachings. The propositions indicate that the *alumbrados* seem to have favored *dejamiento* and relied exclusively on the inner guidance of the Holy Spirit. Given these beliefs and practices, the Church could ill afford to tolerate a spirituality that in its very being leaned dangerously close to what most Spaniards regarded as the worst evil of all—Lutheranism.

The following propositions taken from the Edict of Toledo illustrate how the *alumbrados* rejected the Church and celebrated the individual as God's true tabernacle:

Proposition Four: If the creature did what he ought to do, God came more completely into the soul of man than in the host, for the host was a bit of matter whereas man was in His likeness.

Proposition Nine: The love of God in man is God, and people who abandon themselves to this love of God cannot commit mortal or venial sins.

Proposition Eleven: After one abandons himself to God, abandonment alone is sufficient to save his soul; it is not necessary to fast or perform works of mercy.

Proposition Twenty: Prayer must be mental rather than vocal; prayer in church was an obstacle and God was not served by vocal prayer; people were not to pray using their mouth.

In general the propositions lauded secular over monastic life, claiming, for example, that spouses were more intimately united with God in the marriage act than in prayer.[11] With Sor María's love of the eucharist, her insistence on penitence and mortification of the flesh, and commitment to monasticism, she does not seem to fit comfortably within the ranks of the *alumbrados* even though scholars have tried to place her there. It deserves mentioning at this point that the historian Menéndez Pelayo, who was largely responsible for associating Sor María with the *alumbrados,* found the *alumbrados* altogether reprehensible. Not content to condemn the *alumbrados* for what he maintained was an indisputable connection with the medieval Waldensians, Beghards and *fratricellos*—none of them any good by his measure—he went so far as to harken back to the age of Indian pantheism and Buddhism and with manifest disapproval set the Spanish heretics in a tradition whose goal he said was "the death and absolute annihilation of individual conscience."[12] Sor María is mentioned in the same breath with these thoroughly despicable types, although Menéndez Pelayo does not consider her heretical but only a fanatic and illuminative woman.[13]

At any rate, a comparison of the propositions and Sor María's writings reveals how far apart the *alumbrados* and the Beata were. Consider their respective attitudes toward meditation on the humanity of Jesus Christ.

Proposition Twelve states that when they were in *dejamiento* the *alumbrados* were not to do anything, lest they put an obstacle in the way of what God wished to effect in them; they were not to be occupied in anything created or even think about the humanity of Christ for that could hinder abandonment in God. According to the twenty-second proposition, the *alumbrados* considered it a defect to think about the passion of the Lord; in fact, one of their women had whipped her servant for having wept over the passion. Proposition Forty-two denies the need for any intermediary whatsoever between the soul and God, including the humanity of Jesus Christ; little devotions on the passion and readings about it are to be given up as hindrances to the soul.

Even a cursory reading of Sor María's *Book of Prayer* is enough to prove that she was nothing if not ardently devoted to meditation on the passion of Jesus Christ; enraptured, she would act out the passion in detail and take the parts of the central characters and even speak in the person of Jesus Christ. In the "Contemplation While Enraptured on Easter Sunday" Sor María enacts a dialogue between Jesus and his Mother after he has died on the cross as well as one with Jesus and Mary Magdalen and another with Jesus and two of his disciples. Interspersed are exhortations for Christians to see and feel Jesus's suffering and to realize that personal sin is the reason why the precious body suffers so horribly.

The blood of the Crucified Christ is a potent image in the Beata's contemplation, for the shedding of the precious liquid is pain, yes, but also the source of strength and healing. As Sor María exclaims in the image of music from a contemplation brought on while hearing a clavichord, "What sin put out of tune, Your blood tuned." (00)

The importance of the cross is another source of disagreement between Sor María and the *alumbrados.* In Proposition Thirteen, which treats of exterior acts, a certain person reportedly was reproached for having knelt before the cross, while in the twenty-fourth a preacher was said to advise that it was not necessary to adore the cross because it was only a piece of wood. The view that the cross was nothing but a piece of wood and thus not appropriate for worship is also the subject of the eighteenth proposition.

For Sor María the cross was her ground of being and she enjoins us over and over to surrender to the cross of Jesus. In a fragment of revelations not included in *The Book of Prayer,* Sor María speaks in the person of Jesus:

> Thus if they [men] consider how I was cruelly tormented in all My members on the cross, they may be converted and say: "Woe is me, for all my life I have gravely offended You in all my members! I am the one who continually crucifies You." And if they consider how they offended Me in all their members, then they will receive My cross and they will see how I took their place, suffering for them grave torments in all My members.[14]

Out of rapture the Beata is no less devoted to the cross; in her letter of consolation to a gentleman of Segovia she urges him to clasp the cross, "so rich, strong and powerful," and to hold tightly to it because it alone is "our guardian, support and protection against the fierce dragons and basilisks that prowl about to devour us." The cross, she continues, "is our entire strength, our entire joy, that which consoles and accompanies our solitude, that which gives hope to those who live without it." By the cross passions are overcome and "we walk securely wherever we go." (180)

A troublesome area for the Church was the attitude of the *alumbrados* toward works, including public and private acts of reverence, both of which are covered in Proposition Thirteen: outer acts of prayer are not necessary; people need not show humility at the name of Jesus by bowing their head; nor must they show reverence to the blessed sacrament in procession through the streets. Other propositions, such as the fourteenth, address specific acts: to rise for the reading of the gospel and to make other signs and humiliations is nothing more than playing in church. Again, as in Proposition Twenty-seven: what is the good of excommunications, fasts and abstinences since they hinder the soul which must be free? Proposition Nineteen covers a variety of specific acts: what spiritual good comes from blessing oneself with holy water, striking the breast penitentially, kissing the ground at the words *incarnatus est?*

The Beata's life and teachings vigorously countermand the attitude of the *alumbrados:* not only did Sor María fast, abstain and otherwise mortify herself, but she enthusiastically counseled others to labor hard in order to cleanse the garden of the soul. In a beautiful passage she expresses in the image of tilling the soul the need for outer works of penitence and devotion:

> Woe to us if we do not realize that our gardens are dry and overgrown with weeds! Why, then, do we not realize that we have but a single hour of life and if we leave untended the weeds within, they will sink their roots and habits of bad behavior so deeply we will not be able to pull them out later? (159)

The fragment of Sor María's *Revelations* is such a convincing expression of the need to labor for the sake of the soul that it is cited in full as a way of summarizing the profound difference between the Beata and the *alumbrados.* First the Lord speaks through the Beata and then she speaks in her own person:

> Whenever men do not have other matters, I want them to occupy their time reading or praying, though it pleases me more if they pray, because in prayer the soul tastes My sweetness or gentleness. And what they think about or say in prayer is to be done lovingly: and the words are to be few and spoken attentively and devoutly. . . .
>
> In reading they are to be in this manner so that the reading is from divine scripture and other books for the purpose of the soul's illness. And they are to try to understand what they read and reflect on it so that they seek nothing except Me.
>
> In this way, when they leave holy reading and devout prayer for the matters and works of charity, they will draw from My heart and take with them My divine love with which to communicate and treat and converse with creatures without dispute and accomplish their other matters with much edification. For those who do not receive from Me are unable by themselves to do any good for themselves, still less for others. . . .
>
> The purpose of our divine vocation, the call to the school of religion, is none other than to die, interiorly and exteriorly, completely to this world and ourselves, and to go to God alone; and so that we may know that just as we change from the clothing of the exterior world to the sackcloth of religion, so we are to strip ourselves bare of all things of this world, always remembering that we are dust and vile ashes before the Lord; and we are to have continually in our body the mortification of the cross, deeds which are true copies of our Redeemer and Master; and so that together we may die in the same interior way to our unruly affections and desires, killing our own wills and all our self-love and intelligence and all the other vices of the body, and perfectly denuded and shorn of the old man, we may put on the new man.

> The canonical hours are prayer that they owe Me by obligation. And they are to say them when they are the most quiet and unoccupied, and they are to say them with the mouth and heart. And it would please Me very much if before and after each of the hours they would raise their hearts to think about what I suffered for them at each hour.
>
> If they see flesh, let them remember how I put it on for their salvation, so that they might dress themselves in Me and die totally to all fleshly things; and if they happen to love flesh, let it be only that which I put on that they might put on Me. If they see a beam of wood, let them remember the cross on which I died to kill death in them and give them life in Me. If they see trees, may they see how they yield fruit and flowers, and the same with all things I created; and may they see that they alone are the ones that yield no good fruit on their own.
>
> We always ought to be in prayer for that is what most pleases the Lord; and if not, in devout reading of Holy Scripture or other books that they read for that purpose. And in them [books] we ought to learn nothing except how to find Christ, for from His heart we attract to ourselves and receive the love and grace of His which we transmit to our neighbors when we consent to their conversation and need. Otherwise we can only give and communicate the venom and poison of our iniquity with which we are filled.
>
> Oh how misfortunate are all those, especially religious, and how blameworthy before the Lord those who through negligence permit sins to rust and grow in their heart and conscience; rather they should continually labor, without ceasing, to have them bright and clean and clear, as do those who try to have their swords very polished and clean and burnished, that in this way they may deserve to be the temples and mansions of the Lord.[15]

Sor María thus honors in her writings religious orders, vocal and mental prayer, devotional reading, penitence, mortification of the flesh and meditation on the life and passion of Jesus Christ. She also reveres the Church in its saints and Blessed Mother and she respects its ecclesiastical structure. The woman whose spiritual portrait emerges from this comparison is no relative of the *alumbrados* but an obedient daughter of the Church. It is true that she was affected by the winds of religious controversy that swept across Europe and Spain and that pushed her and her associates to the edge of schism in their avid quest for inner reform. And it is equally true that she appears radical in her piety, raptures, austerities and prophecies. But she was not a theological rebel. The analysis of the content and style of her *Book of Prayer* in the following chapter will show that her spirituality was in the mainstream of a tradition that watered the inner gardens of a Catherine of Siena, a Teresa of Ávila and a John of the Cross.

Chapter Five

The Book of Prayer

Cajetan may have assigned Sor María to permanent residence in her monastery, but his directive of September 1509 did not consign her to obscurity. *The Book of Prayer* is evidence that the Beata's fame continued after the conclusion of the examination, while the content of the introductory material, which accounts for about one-third of the text, proves that controversy about Sor María was far from settled.

The text must have been arranged between 1512, when Vitoria wrote to Cisneros explaining that he was staying on at Aldeanueva in order to transcribe Sor María's contemplations as the cardinal had requested, and 1518, which is the probable date of publication. There are three separate references in the text that suggest the selections were compiled and the introductory material composed after the examination of 1509–10. In the first reference the author of the summary of her life remarks on the goodness of Sor María's life and works "which has been proven by many witnesses in the proceedings that have already taken place against her." (131) A second statement mentions "the proceedings against her" (138), and in the third the editor reminds the reader that "the affairs as well as the person of this handmaid of God have been impugned by many powerful people" but "they have been proven and declared holy and good." (142) The text had to have been composed before Cardinal Adrian, to whom the work is dedicated, was elected to the papacy in 1522.

Less clear is the identity of the person or persons who arranged the four selections attributed to Sor María and who wrote the introduction, which is made up of a prologue addressed to Cardinal Adrian, an explanation of the division of the text, a summary of the Beata's life and a note to the readers. The authorship and content of the introduction is our first consideration in this discussion of the text.

1. Introduction: Authorship and Text

The laudatory tone and intimate detail of the "Summary of Her Virtuous and Perfect Life" suggest that the unidentified editor was a close associate of Sor María. The two possibilities that come to mind are her confessor, Diego de Vitoria, and the man who acted as her defense counsel at the examination, Antonio de la Peña. Both men were in good standing with Cisneros; Vitoria had transcribed the contemplations at the prelate's behest and Antonio de la Peña's translation of the writings of Catherine of Siena was an enterprise ordained by the cardinal.

It is tempting to name Antonio de la Peña as editor on the basis of references to Catherine of Siena in the "Summary," but Vitoria must also have known about the Italian saint, though perhaps not as surely as the translator did. The two men would have been in a position to familiarize Sor María with Catherine and encourage her "to imitate and follow the habit, life and penitence of St. Catherine insofar as she is able and God so desires." (135)

One method that may disclose clues to the editor's identity is to compare the language of the "Summary" with the second defense prepared by Antonio de la Peña. Even in English there is a sense of similarity in the wording and content. From the defense: "The said Sor María at a tender age made and was accustomed to making severe penitences and abstinences and fasts and scourges to the point of shedding considerable blood. She was charitable, devout and merciful to poor and afflicted Christians, and in this she was fervent." (#3) From the "Summary:" "As a child she began to serve God in wondrous ways: she suffered acute hunger; she fasted frequently for long periods during which she ate nothing for months and subsisted on only roots and herbs for other months; she patiently and joyfully endured intense cold, poverty, austerities, scourges and very rigorous penitence. . . ." (131) Again, from the defense: "For love of God and with desire to serve Him, she keeps some children" . . . "giving them a very holy and very religious upbringing, teaching them to serve God and doing all she can to see that they learn to read and write and know grammar and to be devout, punishing them, like a mother, when they make a mistake." (#29) From the "Summary:" "Not counting the expense of caring for many other poor women and men, both children and old people, whom she makes study and whom she educates in religion, she spends a great deal on the religious and gives many alms publicly and secretly." (142) The content, wording and admiring tone of the two texts are similar with respect to other topics such as her good influence on secular and religious men and women and the foundation of Aldeanueva.

The evidence of such similarity is not conclusive evidence that Antonio de la Peña is the unnamed editor, for Vitoria and others might have had access to the written defense, in which case the unknown editor-author could have been influenced not only by the points of the defense but also by their phrasing. For lack of firm evidence the question of the editor's identity must go unanswered for now.

The first part of the introductory material is a prologue in which the editor presents to the book's recipient, Cardinal Adrian,[1] an eloquent statement of belief in the holiness of Sor María and the truth of her teaching. The writer forcefully contrasts the acquired learning of scholarly men and the learning infused in the Beata by the Holy Spirit, reminding his reader of the Church's long-standing respect for the inspired teaching of her unlettered holy men and women. He does not negate the truth and efficacy of acquired learning but he recognizes the superiority of infused knowing and loving in the relationship of the two kinds of learning. The distinction had been central to Catholic theology for centuries before Sor María and in the sixteenth century it would receive the attention of Francisco de Osuna as well as John of the Cross in his *Ascent of Mount Carmel* and *Dark Night of the Soul.*

The orthodoxy of the Beata's teaching and her exemplary humility are reasons for the editor's conviction that she was God's greatest and most enlightened handmaid among women living at that time. After establishing her spiritual authority and moral rectitude, the editor focuses on himself and his reason for printing the work at hand. The tone is tactful and clever as he removes responsibility for the decision from himself to Cardinal Adrian, who has the authority after all to order the book burned and his servant punished if it is not all he is proclaiming it to be; the implication is that the book is altogether orthodox and the Beata thoroughly praiseworthy in virtue and wisdom.

The eloquence and stratagems of the trained apologist characterize the "Summary of Her Virtuous and Perfect Life" as well as the "Prologue." Most points on the Beata's behalf appeared already in the defense although there are emphases and material that are not in strict conformity with the preceding document; the argument in support of her fasting, for example, occupies a longish thirty-percent of the "Summary." The defense is two-pronged. First, the writer defuses the criticism that Sor María with her excessive fasting sought to outdo Jesus, the Blessed Mother and the apostles who did not go without food or drink, and he reconciles her rigorous fasting with the teaching that "the disciple or servant must not be greater than his lord and teacher." (132) Second, he adduces examples from the Bible and Christian tradition to prove that prolonged fast and abstinence characterize many holy men and women whom the Church praised as good and did not condemn for behavior that might be considered in competition with their Lord's. He concludes the litany of fasting men and women with the theological injunction not to judge holiness by fasting but rather by charity, and the observation that by all accounts Sor María was a woman of inspiring charity.

The unusually long defense of Sor María's eating habits implies that her fasting had become even more rigorous after the examination and as a result it incurred even graver doubts and sharper criticism. The bitter division of opinion about her holiness on the basis of fasting bears out recent studies on the eating habits of saintly women in the Middle Ages, which show that attitudes toward fasting women were often contradictory.[2] On the one hand a woman was acclaimed saintly for a practice that set her apart precisely because it was radically different and on the other hand the radical nature of the practice made her an easy target for criticism and set her up for charges of fakery and delusion. There was persuasive evidence in both directions. The examples of holy women who fasted were plentiful, but cases of pretense were also widely documented. Magdalena de la Cruz was a nun in Córdoba who was hailed throughout Spain as an ecstatic oracle, but she confessed under questioning (reportedly she confessed of her own free will) that she had acted under the devil's influence for forty years. Equally notorious was the case of María de la Visitación in Lisbon who finally confessed that she herself had painted the marks of Christ's wounds on her body. Given these and other cases of fraud, the Church was inclined to exercise caution rather than hastily accede to claims of supernatural gifts only to discover later that they were forgeries.

Such situations as the ones cited above raised significant questions about how to imitate Jesus Christ and strive for Christian perfection. One modern scholar has shown that the answer of medieval holy women was to plunge into suffering in order to share experientally in the passion of their Savior.[3] Sor María seems to have followed in this tradition, abetted in her effort by the redoubtable example of Catherine of Siena.

In the matter of the genuineness of Sor María's fasting, the statements by the Beata and witnesses at the examination do not indicate that pretense or trickery were involved. The testimony is, after all, that she was unable to hold food on her stomach and that the process of elimination had stopped. The breakdown of her digestive system seems to be a reliable indicator that in fact she did not eat; whether abstinence originally or ever was self-induced or given by the Lord is a question that we simply cannot answer.

It is reasonable to suppose that what began as a conscious effort to control eating for the purpose of disciplining the body, which in turn was supposed to strengthen virtue and intensify awareness of the suffering Christ, developed into a behavior of such proportions as to cause serious damage to the body. As to the supernatural origin of the phenomenon, reason can only observe and assess evidence and infer conclusions on that basis. From the observation that the Beata suffered illnesses that several witnesses thought were brought on by epilepsy or problems with her heart, it is plausible to attribute her inability to retain what she swallowed to physical ailments. Another observation is that some witnesses testified to the unwavering conviction that prolonged fasting was a supernatural gift bestowed on her by God. Unless one ventures onto the slippery terrain of psychoanalyzing the witnesses, the only safe conclusion this testimony yields is that some people believed her fasting and abstinence were God-given. Thus the situation is that the Beata was frequently ill, she fasted and abstained for exceedingly long periods of time, and some people thought that her illnesses and fasts were causally connected while others professed belief in their divine origin.

The criticism which the editor answers in the "Summary" appears to be directed not so much to phenomena like fasting as to the praise and fame that accrued to the Beata on their account; he is mindful of the Biblical injunction not to praise and magnify a person in her lifetime. At this point the editor seems to have chosen as the best defense a strong offense; he pushes the criticism and burden of proof away from Sor María and onto her detractors. A hint of this shift appears in the defense when Antonio de la Peña denounces those who feel scandalized by the Beata,[4] but it is the "Summary" that soundly challenges her critics to examine their souls: "Who will make sure and certain," the editor asks, "that those who obstinately insist on believing and speaking in this way are not deceived by the devil?" He continues: "For if they believe that this religious and handmaid of God by whom the enemy has been defeated so many times—she whose body lives and is sustained beyond all natural power and whose soul is always filled with spiritual joy and is unwaveringly serene—can be deceived by the devil, how much more can those who think ill of her be deceived?" (140)

It is not the Beata who is blameworthy but her detractors who fail to humble themselves, recognize their sins and do penance. (143) If they acted as they should, the key of humility would open their understanding. And if they but came into the presence of this remarkable woman, they would feel inspired to repent and amend their lives. (143) The tone is equally forceful as he accuses her critics of blasphemy for attributing her great works to the devil rather than God:

> . . . I fail to know or understand how a Christian does not commit blasphemy if he attributes evil to God and good to the devil when he says that this is the deception of the devil rather than the grace of the Holy Spirit, which it is and must be believed to be so for many obvious reasons. (139–40)

Changing tactics and tone, the editor reminds his readers that even if we have doubts we are obliged to assume the best about our neighbors for "human law assumes as much while divine law ordains us to believe thus and to interpret doubtful cases in the best, most salutary light." (139) Thus the editor has placed a burden of guilt on Sor María's critics that includes failure of Christian compassion, deception by the devil and blasphemy! These sinners he also judges unworthy to hear and understand the Beata's words. In the brief note to the readers he advises that "only those who already may feel their spirit separated from the affections of the world and joined to God in true love and holy fear will be able to appreciate and judge from reading this little work." (145)

2. The Theology of the *Book*

Whereas the analysis of Sor María and the *alumbrados* concentrated on what her theology was not, the point of the present discussion is to clarify what it was. With that purpose in mind, this explanation is first necessary: Sor María did not compose theology but rather she expressed themes that have theological implications and that bear comparison with mystical theology. Whether she speaks in or out of ecstasy there is theological consistency to the selections contained in the little book, as she expresses the journey of the soul to union with God through the themes of love, sin and salvation.

Love is the ground of being: God's love for creation and her, Jesus's love as manifested in his life and death, her love for God and others. Life is growth in love as the soul becomes more and more aware of God's love for her and hers for him. In her understanding that love in God and through God is the purpose of life and the means to its realization, Sor María is in the tradition of affective mystics who speak of mystical union in terms of the union of wills and who employ the language of human love to express the conformity of divine and human wills as the seal of spiritual marriage.

Although there was an abundance of affective mystics before Sor María, it is especially in Franciscan spirituality, which is infused with the compassion of St. Francis, that the affective way stands out. The Dominicians, however, also had their affective mystics, as the life and writings of Catherine of Siena reveal. The affective thrust to Catherine's mysticism appears immediately in the "Prologue" to *The Dialogue* in her beautiful statement that "by love's affection the soul becomes another himself [Christ]."[5] Christ says through Catherine that souls "who are clothed in the wedding garment of charity" are united with Him "through love." (p. 26) "'So I say, if you should ask me who they are, said the gentle loving Word, 'that they are another me, for they have lost and drowned their own will and have clothed themselves and united themselves and conformed themselves with mine.'" (p. 26) Thus it is true, the saint concludes, "that the soul is united to God through love's affection." (p. 26)

In sixteenth-century Spain, affective mysticism found ardent disciples in the Franciscan Osuna and in later Carmelites, who drew heavily on Franciscan sources. Osuna traces the journey to God in love in his *Third Spiritual*

Alphabet, advising in the twelfth of the book's twenty-two treatises that the soul was given the two wings of understanding and will to fly to God. Although "some still presume and strive to reach the repose of contemplation by fluttering the left wing of understanding," Osuna says, "they are like a rower who tries to put into a quiet port with just one oar or a swimmer endeavoring to reach shore using but one arm." The purpose of his chapter is to counsel people "not to assume that they can attain the repose they desire through the understanding, which is to employ the left wing, but to realize they must use the right wing [love], which is that of tasting."[6]

Teresa of Ávila and John of the Cross also speak of mystical union in terms of the will. Midway in the journey through the interior castle of the soul, Teresa describes the will in conformity with God's will as if it were wax awaiting the impress;

> That soul has now delivered itself into His hands and His great love has so completely subdued it that it neither knows nor desires anything save that God shall do with it what He wills. Never, I think, will God grant this favour save to the soul which He takes for His very own. His will is that, without understanding how, the soul shall go thence sealed with His seal. In reality, the soul in that state does no more than the wax when a seal is impressed upon it—the wax does not impress itself; it is only prepared for the impress: that is, it is soft—and it does not even soften itself so as to be prepared; it merely remains quiet and consenting. Oh, goodness of God, that all this should be done at Thy cost! Thou dost require only our wills and dost ask that Thy wax may offer no impediment.[7]

The image of the bride and bridegroom wedded is beautifully expressive of the intimacy of soul and God in the delicate loving of the seventh mansions of the *Interior Castle:* "For He has been pleased to unite Himself with His creature in such a way that they have become like two who cannot be separated from one another."[8]

The most sublime expression and lucid explanation of the union of wills are the poetry and prose of John of the Cross.

In chapter five of the second book of the *Ascent of Mount Carmel,* John draws the distinction between the union of substance and the union of likeness; the first is that by which we exist and the second is that by which we are transformed by love into Love:

> In order, then, to understand what is meant by this union whereof we are treating, it must be known that God dwells and is present substantially in every soul, even in that of the greatest sinner in the world. And this kind of union is ever wrought between God and all the creatures, for in it He is preserving their being: if union of this kind were to fail them, they would at once become annihilated and would cease to be. And so, when we speak of union of the soul with God, we speak not of this substantial union which is continually being wrought, but of the union and transformation of the soul with God, which is not being wrought continually, but only when there is produced that likeness that comes from love; we shall therefore term this the union of likeness, even as that other union is called substantial or essential. The former is natural, the latter supernatural. And the latter comes to pass when the two wills—namely that of the soul and that of God—are conformed together in one and there is naught in the one that is repugnant to the other. And thus, when the soul rids itself totally of that which is repugnant to the Divine will and conforms not with it, it is tranformed in God through love.[9]

The journey to union in love of which Catherine, Osuna, Teresa and John sing begins for Sor María when the soul acknowledges that her will is turned away from God and when she is impelled by love to begin changing her attitude and behavior. "Since my will's disorders," she laments, "which separate me from You want to separate my soul from You, when will my soul cry out and call to You that they do not separate her from You?" (148) The intensity of desire bursts forth in her exclamation that she longs to be "inebriated" in God's love. (148)

But desire must be translated into action. Thus Sor María begins to till and clear the garden of her soul and to exhort her listeners to grasp the hoe which the Lord also offers them:

> What is the hoe He orders us to grasp? It is penitence by which we clear the garden of the good conscience. And the channel through which water enters this garden to make flowers beautiful and the grasses of virtues green, that channel is our will that is conformed to His will, held and closely attached to Him. It is, also, when the soil is well tilled and our passions are conquered that the purity of the precious hoe keeps watch and tills the garden of the quiet soul so that it is continually refreshed and watered with the Beloved's love and warmth. (158–59)

The passage is also noteworthy in its use of water as the image for God's love and the means by which the soul nourishes herself; the image anticipates Teresa's celebrated description of the four waters by which the soul grows in love for God.[10]

In her counsel to grasp the hoe of the Lord, Sor María reveals another connection with the Christian mystical tradition that was to flower profusely in her century: her spirituality is Christ-centered, with special emphasis on the Jesus who suffered and died to save sinners. In the contemplation inspired by the music of a clavichord, Sor María plays on images of Christ's suffering. She says in the person of Jesus:

> "My blood will be shed for you so you may have a precious bath of charity in it and love in which to cleanse and wash yourselves. It is not that I am unable to rear you in grace and sustain you in grace without having to shed My blood, but it was necessary for your sake that I come down among you, become a man like you, and shed My blood for you so that My love (which I showed you by doing this) might raise you up more for Me and make you more conformed to Me and thus enhance your happiness with Me." (172–73)

The theme of the passion as a revelation of God's love is also at the heart of the letter of consolation:

> In His immense and most excellent kindness He created us, and with amazing love and kindness He freed us by His most sacred passion from the most fierce prisons of self-love and misery. (179)

Sor María's injunction to imitate Jesus clearly reflects the writings of Catherine of Siena and Angela of Foligno and will resonate in the texts of both Osuna and Teresa. Indeed, the images of the soul as garden and watering with the blood of Christ have unmistakable precedent in Catherine's *Dialogue.* In the following passage from *The Dialogue* the images are developed simultaneously to express the need for the soul to labor in her garden in order to nourish moral perfection and to be watered with Christ's saving blood:

> Each of you has your own vineyard, your soul, in which your free will is the appointed worker during this life. Once the time of your life has passed, your will can work neither for good nor for evil; but while you live it can till the vineyard of your soul where I have placed it. This tiller of your soul has been given such power that neither the devil nor any other creature can steal it without the will's consent, for in holy baptism the will was armed with a knife that is love of virtue and hatred of sin. This love and hatred are to be found in the blood. For my only-begotten Son gave his blood for you in death out of love for you and hatred for sin, and through that blood you receive life in holy baptism.[11]

Blood was as consuming an image for Angela of Foligno as it was for Catherine and would be for Sor María:

> While I was in prayer, keeping vigil, Christ showed himself to me on the cross with such clarity—that is, that he gave me greater knowledge of him. And then he called me and said I should put my mouth to the wound in his side. And it seemed to me that I saw and drank his blood flowing freshly from his side. And I was given to understand that by this he would cleanse me. And at this I began to feel great joy, although when I thought about the passion I felt sadness. And I prayed the Lord that he would cause me to shed all my blood for his love, just as he had done for me.[12]

Francisco de Osuna is not as dramatic in references to blood as the Italian women visionaries but he does encourage us to imitate the Sacred Humanity while recognizing that "the task that most frightens human beings is that of following Jesus Christ."[13] But Christians must follow Christ as best they can, not only in success but also adversity. "Brothers," exhorts Osuna, "if we truly wish to follow Christ, let us emulate the apostles and leave behind the nets of worldly concerns in which the devil ensnares us."[14] Sor María's language is strikingly similar as she urges us to consider "the entangled ties of this sad, deceitful world and its captivity" and counsels the Segovian gentleman to whom she writes to "clasp the cross, so rich, strong and powerful, of Jesus Christ crucified." (180)

Teresa of Ávila was so devoted to the Sacred Humanity that she prayed by visualizing and reflecting on an event in the passion:

> By meditation I mean prolonged reasoning with the understanding, in this way. We begin by thinking of the favour which God bestowed upon us by giving us His only Son; and we do not stop there but proceed to consider the mysteries of His whole glorious life. Or we begin with the prayer in the Garden and go on rehearsing the events that follow until we come to the Crucifixion. Or we take one episode of the Passion—Christ's arrest, let us say—and go over this mystery in our mind, meditating in detail upon the points in it which we need to think over and to try to realize, such as the treason of Judas, the flight of the Apostles, and so on. This is an admirable and a most meritorious kind of prayer.[15]

Even when Teresa was far along the path to union and experienced the extraordinary phenomena characteristic of the higher reaches of her inner journey, she did not renounce meditation on the Sacred Humanity as some writers advised, but rather she insisted on the benefits of its practice:

> You will also think that anyone who enjoys such sublime favours will not engage in meditation on the most sacred Humanity of Our Lord Jesus Christ, because by that time he will be wholly proficient in love. . . . Some souls

> also imagine that they cannot dwell upon the Passion, in which case they will be able still less to meditate upon the most sacred Virgin and the lives of the saints, the remembrance of whom brings us such great profit and encouragement. I cannot conceive what they are thinking of; for, though angelic spirits, freed from everything corporeal, may remain permanently enkindled in love, this is not possible for those of us who live in this mortal body . . . the last thing we should do is to withdraw of set purpose from our greatest help and blessing, which is the most sacred Humanity of Our Lord Jesus Christ.[16]

Teresa's insistence on the need to meditate on the Sacred Humanity was also a direct refutation of the quietism of the *alumbrados* that urged abandonment to God and renouncing active devotion and works of charity.

Although the soul must actively pray and labor to imitate Jesus Christ in tilling the inner garden, the hard work bears unspeakably precious fruit, for as Sor María says, the Lord himself enters the garden to till and water it. The channel through which God's waters flow into the soul is the "will that is conformed to His will, held and closely attached to Him." (159) The language of this passage and elsewhere implies that the conforming of the will to God's will is a divine act. The Beata says that "the garden cannot be watered except through the channel of the individual will that is in conformity with the will of the One who has the sweet water to refresh and gladden it." (159) And she wonders "who with purity of conscience will not keep watch over the channel of the will that is closely conformed to God's will so that the water of love and fervor will not be lacking in the soul's garden?" (160)

Thus the soul journeys toward loving union with God by her active work in the garden as she meditates and does penitence and acts of charity and more importantly by the secret watering and tilling that God does on her behalf in his infinite love and mercy. In short, the journey inward is both active and passive, although the soul ultimately is totally passive as she is transformed by grace so that her will is conformed with the will of God in the act and condition that is known as the spiritual marriage.

Although Sor María herself experienced raptures, visions, miraculous communion and other "consolations" that are familiar from tales of medieval and Renaissance saints, but which were viewed by writers like the Dominican Ferrer and the Carmelite John of the Cross as possible hindrances rather than helps along the inner way, she neither yearns for them nor considers them essential for spiritual growth. On the contrary, her impassioned plea is to "run to seek Him in your heart" and she advises that "Your will is always conformed to His if you do not long for consolations." (162) Rather than longing for consolations, the Beata yearns to labor in her garden, cling to the cross and love God ever more purely.

Had the examiners considered only the words contained in this little volume, had they not known they were uttered in ecstasy by a woman, and had they not faced the accusations and suspicions of Sor María's critics, their work would have been eased, for they would have seen at once that Sor María spoke sound Catholic doctrine. And mystical theologians would have recognized in her words traditional teaching about the path to union and the nature of that union as the conforming of the divine and human wills in the spiritual marriage.

3. The *Book* as Text

Sor María did not write *The Book of Prayer* in the sense of setting pen to paper. She was unable to do that, of course, because she was illiterate. Nor did she miraculously learn to read and write, as Catherine of Siena reputedly did. There is no evidence that Sor María ever learned to read or write or that she regarded herself as a writer, as did many medieval visionary women for whom writing and dictating was a self-conscious act.[17]

In a statement given at the examination in 1509, Diego de Vitoria described the method of composition that eventually resulted in *The Book of Prayer*. It will be recalled that Cisneros had charged Vitoria with writing down the Beata's words so that he might have them for his own instruction and that Vitoria had used this reason in a letter of 1512 that he wrote to the cardinal to justify his remaining at Aldeanueva in Sor María's company. Vitoria explained in his statement that sometimes he would wait a day or more before he wrote down what he had heard. If there were two or three or even ten people in attendance, they would confer among themselves about what she said. The point of such a conference was to reach an agreement about what the Beata had said, although they did not always agree on the exact meaning of her words. Vitoria added that he did not want the examiners to give undue faith to his own writing because he was aware that not all of them understood things in the same way.[18] His statement raises perplexing questions about the process. How faithful were Vitoria and others in remembering the Beata's words? Did they consciously alter her utterances? Did the Beata herself listen to their transcriptions and in turn modify them? Since there are no other references to the act of transcription in the available documents, these questions must remain as hauntingly unanswered as others.

There are intriguing hints in the testimony of the witnesses at the examination that Sor María was aware to some degree of what she was saying. In the context of the examination, the testimony that Sor María would change words while speaking in rapture, as if she were trying to suit them to her listener, tended to discredit the genuineness of her ecstasies. In terms of the creative process, however, the statement suggests that she was more conscious of composing than might have been supposed.

The reason for attempting to define the process of composition is that somehow the question must be faced of whether the *Book* is really Sor María's creation. Furthermore, is it legitimate to regard her *Book* as a text and subject it to literary analysis?

There is precedent at least in part for assuming that words uttered or written down in ecstasy constitute a text. Catherine of Siena's writing is a case in point. Her biographers testify that a mystical inspiration caused her to begin composition of *The Dialogue:*

> So about two years before her death, such a clarity of Truth was revealed to her from heaven that Catherine was constrained to spread it abroad by means of writing, asking her secretaries to stand ready to take down whatever came from her mouth as soon as they noticed that she had gone into ecstasy. Thus in a short time was composed a certain book that contains a dialogue between a soul who asks the Lord four questions, and the Lord himself who replies to the soul, enlightening her with many useful truths.[19]

Contemporary accounts support the claim that much of the book "involved a great deal of dictation on her part while she was in ecstasy."[20] Her biographer, Caffarini, testified:

> I say also that I have very often seen the virgin in Siena, especially after her return from Avignon, rapt beyond her senses, except for speech, by which she dictated to various writers in succession sometimes letters and sometimes the book, in different times and in different places, as circumstances allowed. Sometimes she did this with her hands crossed on her breast as she walked about the room; sometimes she was on her knees or in other postures; but always her face was lifted toward heaven.[21]

Modern scholars believe that Catherine's role in the creative process was larger than her contemporaries asserted and there is even evidence that she wrote some of *The Dialogue* and edited it as well.[22] However much Catherine may have composed in ecstasy critics have not hesitated to study her writings as literary texts.

Teresa of Ávila is another visionary who reportedly wrote as if inspired by the Holy Spirit. Even though Teresa did not regard herself as a writer, critics have been no less reluctant to apply the term "text" to her writings than they have been to name Catherine's works literature and to assess them with the tools of literary criticism.

Although the examples of Teresa and Catherine—to name only two of many ecstatic visionary women who wrote while divinely inspired—are reason to validate Sor María's *Book* as text, the case finally must be argued on its own merit.

The point is that a book exists that has historically been ascribed to Sor María. To insist out of hand that she herself had to have set pen to paper for her book to qualify as a text is nonsense. It would be equally absurd to question her state of consciousness, as if one could or should establish a scale by which to measure creative awareness. That enterprise would be as irrelevant as questioning an author's intention, sincerity or dependence on drugs.

Given the existence of the *Book*, the issue is how to assess it as a text. Recent scholarship by feminist critics and theoreticians emphasizes that in the case of women's writing it is especially important to set aside methodologies and categories that served a literature canonized by men. The necessary task for the feminist scholar is to identify women's writing; the task has uncovered a bounty of literature in the form of letters, diaries, journals, autobiographies, oral histories and confessional poetry. According to this approach the concept of text is realized in the evidence; the feminist critic chancing upon Sor María's *Book* would not be concerned about identifying it as a text according to an established category. She would not ask a question like "Is the *Book* mystical literature?" because for her the value of a work does not reside in its fidelity to existent models. Rather, the feminist scholar asks whether the book reveals women's experience. Her question assumes a correspondence of text and experience and bears the further assumption that the form is textual by the fact that it reveals women's experience. From this perspective the *Book* of Sor María is a text because it yields "evidence of women's consciousness and expression."[23] A program that constructs "a female framework for the analysis of women's literature" and develops "new models based on the study of female experience"[24] would undoubtedly include Sor María's book as a text.

There is more to feminist literary criticism than researching sources of women's experience. The nettling question is whether to assign artistic value to women's texts by criteria other than the one of experience. And if so, what would be the criteria? In other words, can judgments be made about

Sor María's *Book* other than to name it a literary text on the grounds that it discloses a woman's "consciousness and expression"? Feminist critics do not offer a unanimous answer to the questions, nor do they even agree that pluralism is the proper attitude toward methodology. Their burgeoning literature is clear evidence, however, that in practice the questions remain vitally open to discussion. Since my inclination is to the pluralist stance,[25] I propose to weave several methodological strands into my own text of literary criticism, beginning with the conventional approach that judges artistry in terms of inner coherence.

The "Contemplation While Enraptured on Easter Sunday," which is the selection from the text that I have chosen to analyze from the point of view of inner coherence, has the markings of dramatic literature: there are three discernible parts that could qualify as acts as well as opening and closing prayers that serve as a prologue and an epilogue in which the themes of sin, penitence, salvation and faith are introduced and resolved. The cast of characters includes the Blessed Mother, Mary Magdalen, the disciples John and Peter and the Beata herself in the roles of protagonist and narrator. The Beata voices the themes in the prayer at the beginning and end while the main characters embody the themes and dramatize the story of salvation accomplished through penitence and faith.

The first act opens as the Beata summons us to see the dolorous Mother of sinners waiting for her Beloved. The silence of her painful waiting is broken by her Son's greeting: '"Oh My sweet mother, you see Me here now risen. Rejoice with Me and in Me for the redemption, which is now accomplished.'" (152) Although Jesus assures his weeping mother that the redemption is accomplished, she does not cease to sorrow for our humanity that is abandoned to anguished darkness with the Lord's departure. Though she begs him to console the disconsolate, he replies that all people must be left to their creatureliness if they are to accept their utter sinfulness and dependence on him.

The dialogue ends when the Beata steps in to praise the Blessed Mother, who endured in sorrow and kept faith alone of all creatures because she alone was untainted by sin. Then Jesus resumes his teaching that his passion must stun all people and cut through their consciousness so sharply that they will strive to put on the new person and prepare themselves for the spiritual rebirth that the resurrection promises. The Beata's ensuing litany of praise in honor of the Blessed Mother brings the first act to a close and serves as a transition to the second act. Implicit in her praise for the "sweet mother of God, stranger to self-love" and "cleansed of self-love" (156) is a lamentation for sinners whose self-love jeopardizes their salvation. Whereas the Blessed Mother exemplifies spiritual perfection in that she loves God for the sake of love and love alone, sinners "seek contemplation with tears and moans only for their own consolation and self-love." (156–57) If sinners abandon self-love and abandon themselves to God, they will be open "to receive from God through His consolation the gift of being made more agreeable to Him and brought into closer conformity with Him so that they will know and be able to do His will, obey Him and thus fulfill the purpose for which He created them." (157)

This speech by Sor María sets the stage for act two and the appearance of Mary Magdalen as the embodiment of the theme of penitence. With the simple question "Whom do you seek, sister?" (157), Sor María introduces Mary Magdalen and establishes a context for the ensuing dialogue with Jesus. As the Blessed Mother was the selfless contemplative soul awaiting her Beloved, Mary Magdalen is the penitent active soul searching for her Lord. Not only does her activity contrast with the quietness of the Blessed Mother, but in her repentence she differs from the sinners whom the Beata reproached for having sought contemplation out of self-love. As the Mother's waiting bore the fruit of Jesus's appearance so Mary Magdalen's work is fruitful in her attitude of complete surrender to Jesus ("'I have already offered myself to Him.... I am already completely His'."[158]) and the revelation of him whom she seeks. Jesus's words beautifully express the intimacy of union that the soul enjoys with God when divine grace conforms the human will with God's will: "'Oh, My daughter, you will love Me and I will love you. You will bear Me within yourself and I will bear you with Me'." (158)

As the Beata reminds her audience, the penitential journey to the marriage of wills is arduous, and we must strive to grasp the hoe that the Beloved gives us and with it root out the weeds of the inner garden, till, water and care for it with unceasing prayer and vigilance. Skillfully weaving images of the soul as garden and images of fertility, Sor María exhorts us finally to "cleanse ourselves of self-will" (161) and accept "grief happily so that He may call and console you" and give you "the power to conform your will to His." (161–62) The exhortation is a gathering up of the themes of penitence and suffering as well as the figures of Mary Magdalen and the Blessed Mother, who asked only that he reveal his will and were not concerned about their own consolation. With her last words in the scene the Beata urges us to "run to seek Him in your heart with those two beloved ones of His" (162), thus bringing together images of running that occur earlier in the text to create a subtle transition from act two to act three. As she built a bridge from the first to the second act with the image of "seeking," she now employs that of "running" to carry us from the second act to the third.

The two figures running are Peter and John who embody the paradoxical theme that there is faith in vacillation. As Jesus revealed himself to the Holy Mother in the context of her sorrow and waiting and to Mary Magdalen in her penitential seeking, he appears now to the disciples in their vacillation and lack of faith. The central dialogue of compassion and forgiveness occupies about two-thirds of the act; its length suggests that God's mercy is vast enough to forgive even those who lose faith. Once again the Beata participates in the dialogue as she explains why Jesus had to reveal himself to the disciples: since the world will not believe women because they are deemed to be inferior in the natural sense, even though they are spiritually equal to men, it is men who must testify that the Lord has truly risen; but since men's faith is not as strong as women's, Jesus had to appear to the men in person and ascend to the Father in full view of them.

Turning to Jesus, the Beata collects the themes of her drama: the need for repentence and tilling the garden, praying for God's help, and the joy of the will that is conformed with God's. Her final supplication is to the Father that he will bestow on her the tears and wisdom he gave the Magdalen and to the Blessed Mother who was exalted in her divine motherhood because she consented to God's will in her will. With startling freshness Sor María expresses the vision of a love wherein God's will and the soul's will are brought into harmony:

> Your goodness and your purity enticed Him to take you for His mother. He desired the enticement, for He fell in love with you; and He fell in love with you for what He had placed of Himself in you. That is why He fell in love with Himself so that by means of you He would be father to us and by means of Him you would be mother to us. (168)

"The Contemplation While Enraptured on Easter Sunday" is coherent in terms of structure, personages, themes and imagery. The text is framed by prayers which at one end introduce the themes and at the other resume and magnify them in the eloquently stunning image of God who is made our Father by his act of making the woman his own mother. Within the frame is a drama in three acts with scenes of prayer, dramatic encounter and three protagonists who incarnate the principal theme of each act: Mary, the figure of sorrow, compassion and faith; Mary Magdalen, that of penitence; John and Peter, together representing lack of faith.

The central drama of each act is an epiphany; considered as a whole the three epiphanies are arranged according to both descending and ascending values. With respect to the spiritual condition of the person to whom Jesus reveals himself, the sequence moves downward from the Blessed Mother to Mary Magdalen to the disciples, but because God's love and mercy is manifestly greater in proportion to the soul's state, the movement is upward as well. The ascending line of divine action expresses the belief that even though the individual clears the garden of the soul, it is God who plants the virtues and urges them to bloom and who brings the human will into conformity with the divine. The ascending-descending sequence of epiphanies further implies a crossing of the lines of action, which in turn symbolizes the interplay of the human and the divine in the soul's journey to union.

The contemplation is the drama of the soul's relationship with God, enacted through Jesus's revelation of himself to the Blessed Mother, Mary Magdalen and the disciples and expressed in the lyricism of prayer, the drama of dialogue and the eloquence of discourse. The drama is a coherent whole in which the individual acts, in their inner structure, mirror the dynamics of the larger unit, for they are unified within themselves and with each other by the repetition of themes, figures and images as well as by the transitional passages that explicitly carry an image or figure from one act to the next.

As impressive as the artistry of the written text is, the impact of the oral text on the listeners must have been astounding. As the Beata summons us to see the Blessed Mother and look at "her clothes and robes bloodied with the most sacred blood of her Beloved" (151); exhorts us to "bear sweet fruit for Him even though it may taste bitter to us" (160); lays bare her soul "alone and unhappy" (147); and begs the Lord to "pity me and sorrow for me" (150), she compellingly draws us into the deep spiritual drama of the soul redeemed by hard work and God's love.

The dramatic quality of the ecstatic representation raises the possibility that Sor María was influenced by the context of liturgical drama that existed in Spain at the time. In Spain, as throughout western Europe, religious drama was born inside the churches as an effort to make Christian mysteries and especially the events of Christmas and Easter immediate to the faithful. The oldest known liturgical play in Spain is found in two manuscripts from the late eleventh century at the Benedictine monastery of Silos near Burgos. Both manuscripts contain a *Visitatio Sepulchri* (Visit to the Sepulchre) that begins with the conventional question of the Easter play: *"Quem queritis in sepulchro hoc, Christicole?"* (Whom do you seek in this sepulchre, Christians?)[26]

Within a century Spanish appears to have supplanted Latin as the language for liturgical drama; the *Play of the Wise Men* from the middle of the twelfth century is evidence that the vernacularization of drama was under way. The scarcity of manuscripts in Latin in Castile for the next three centuries is further proof that Spanish had become the language of liturgical drama as well as of the secular plays that were popular in the Middle Ages.

By the end of the fifteenth century there was an abundance of dramatic material in Spanish that Sor María would have experienced: liturgical drama performed in churches, monasteries and public squares for Easter, Christmas, saints' days and other religious festivals; public processions such as that in honor of the feast of Corpus Christi, which by 1500 had become a popular feature of Spanish religious practice;[27] religious dance, song and pantomime performed in conjunction with the liturgy; and religious plays written by professional dramatists.

Sor María's ecstatic performance of the Easter story falls within the tradition of Spanish and European liturgical drama. The lament of the Blessed Mother, for example, is reminiscent of the *"Planctus Mariae"* ("Mary's Lament"), which liturgically dates from the early days of the Church. Gómez Manrique (1412?–1490?) was one of the first known authors of religious drama to draw on the tradition of the *"Planctus Mariae"* for his *Lamentations Composed for Holy Week,* a tiny drama in which Mary Magdalen stands silent during a dialogue between the Blessed Mother and Saint John. The lamenting Virgin of Sor María's ecstatic representation would have been a familiar figure to an audience nourished on Easter plays like the little one by Gómez Manrique with its conventional *"Planctus Mariae"*:

> Ay, sorrow, sorrow
> For my Son and my Lord!
> I am that Mary
> of the house of David.
> Hear, people, hear
> my great misfortune.
> Ay, sorrow![28]

The Virgin's lament carries through four more strophes, each of which ends with the refrain "Ay, sorrow,".

The next speaker is St. John, who echoes Mary's lament with his own "Ay, sorrow, sorrow/for my cousin and my Lord," and concludes each of the four strophes of his speech with the abbreviated refrain "Ay, sorrow!" after which he addresses Mary Magdalen:

> Oh, sister Magdalen,
> beloved of the Redeemer!
> Who could, with sorrow,
> Alleviate such grave affliction?
> How can the sad, disconsolate one
> who has seen crucified
> the most high King of heaven
> give consolation?
> Ay, sorrow!

He then addresses the Blessed Mother, she answers, and he closes the drama with the exhortation:

> Let us go, let us go to the garden,
> where you will see buried
> your most treasured Son,
> dead by a very crude death.

Although Gómez Manrique's play and Sor María's representation are similar in their theme of sorrow and use of dialogue, the ecstatic representation is obviously longer, more elaborate, and composed of elements that are not found in the earlier drama. The little fifteenth-century piece is entirely in dialogue whereas Sor María's has narration and description as well as dialogue. Nor is there anything in the first play to suggest the various roles that Sor María will enact as she not only portrays the conventional personages of the Easter drama but also inserts herself into the scene as the narrator and a character in her own right. At times she moves almost imperceptibly from one role to the other, though we can imagine that she would have made the transition clear to her audience by the appropriate use of gestures and voice.

By the time Sor María was becoming conscious of the larger world of Spanish society in travels that took her out of her home monastery, such dramatists as Juan del Encina (1468?–1529) were transforming the theatre into an art that was independent of the Church. Although Encina sought new themes and models from the Renaissance theatre of Italy, he did not forsake religious drama: two plays by him, one on the passion and death of the redeemer and the other on the resurrection, were presented for the first time on Holy Thursday and Easter of 1494 in the oratory of his patron and Sor María's famous protector, the duke of Alba.[29] Encina's plays are an undeniable development over the Gómez Manrique play in terms of the larger cast of characters and heightened dramatic tension, but they are remarkably uncomplicated in comparison with Sor María's ecstatic representation.

Whether Sor María attended such performances is not known, but we can be sure that in its processions, festivals, music, liturgies and plays, Spanish Catholicism of her day provided abundant dramatic inspiration. We know from the testimony of witnesses at the proceeding that Sor María's ecstasies were a kind of drama that had cathartic effects on her audience and moved not a few tepid souls to conversion. To what degree she consciously reenacted her own experience of religious drama and dramatic religion is uncertain, but it is clear that Sor María's contemplations were an "ecstatic theatre" in which she was at once author, text and actor.

Sor María's total indentification with her text takes on significance for critical interpretation when it is viewed from the perspective of feminist scholars for whom the body assumes unprecedented importance in the study of literature. One contemporary critic observes that "many women experience their own bodies as the only available medium for their art, with the result that the distance between the woman artist and her art is often radically diminished."[30] The woman artist experiences the diminishment of distance between herself and her art so strongly that it has been said that "she is herself the text."[31] The close identification of the female artist with her art has made of dance an especially acceptable medium because "the body of the dancer becomes an instrument or icon on stage."[32]

"Instrument" and "icon" are appropriate terms for the ecstatic Sor María as she bodily represents the story of the passion, crucifixion and resurrection. In passages like the following, from her prayer before communion in the contemplation on Easter, there is an accumulation of verbs which creates a physical atmosphere wherein the encounter between God and Sor María is bodily as well as spiritual:

> Oh, my God, when I fail to approach You and when I cast You aside, punish and whip me so that You will not demand the final account. If I stumble often and You do not whip me to get me up, then later I will be unable to rise except with much pain even though You may lash me very hard. Then scourge me there so I will not wait to give You the final account. If I stumble and suffer without You, the sad account will be rendered which for me is to remain separated from You and then on judgment day I will have no other account to render. (148)

If Sor María acted out the approaching, casting aside, punishing, whipping, stumbling, rising, lashing and scourging, as I imagine she did, the effect on those in attendance must have been electrifying. To sustain physical and emotional intensity throughout a contemplation of this length while playing the roles of several characters surely left the Beata physically exhausted, even though in her ecstatic state she might not have been fully conscious of expending mental and physical energy.

There were extraordinary demands on Sor María as she employed the dramatic instrument of her body to develop the action, direct the audience's attention now here, now there and form presence out of absence, as when she engages the Blessed Mother in a conversation in which she, the Beata, does all the talking. "Oh sweet Mother of God," she asks, "what do you see in these books?" The Blessed Mother does not reply directly but her response that she has found nothing in the books to reassure her is implicit in the Beata's next words: "Since all the books say that He will rise up, cease weeping now." Before Sor María addresses the Blessed Mother again, she turns to us, saying "Yet she weeps so grievously that the tears of her eyes dampen her clothing." (151)

Had Sor María been acting out a play that she had written and memorized beforehand, the effort of her one-woman performance would have been remarkable enough. That she created the performance from one moment to the next without the benefit of staging to strengthen the artistic illusion is even more remarkable and gives us some understanding of why her viewers described the event as "miraculous" and "inspired."

For the contemporary audience that has only the written text, the act of reading requires imaginative intensity in order to recreate the modulations of voice and bodily movement by which she brought to life the personages of the drama. There is required what has been called an "altered reading attentiveness,"[33] which in the case of the Beata might involve relinquishing our own critical distance from the text and allowing ourselves to be immersed in the flow of her discourse with its shifting voices and immediate physicality.

Even in a contemplation that is not theatre in terms of scenic structure and dramatic personages, the reader is aware of Sor María's body as icon, instrument and text. As she listens to the music of the clavichord, she is inspired to see the soul as a musical instrument and to play on that image the theme that "What sin put out of tune, Your blood tuned." (169) The entire contemplation expresses the soul's journey to realize harmony within herself, with other people and with God by means of her own efforts to tune herself and by God's grace that brings the tuning to perfection.

How sad the Beata is when she realizes that Jesus does not play her sweetly because her sins have dirtied the chords of her soul and how honestly she reproaches herself when she considers that "she herself is a harmony made to be always in tune." (169) Whatever might be her specific sins, she must recognize the attitude that motivates them; hence she reprehends herself because she does not wish to cleanse her soul, but instead goes on clutching "the disorders of my will." (170) Touching on the mystery of desire itself, she confesses that without the "soft hand of Your love and fervor" the music of love lies silent in the heart.(170) Acknowledging her utter helplessness, Sor María sings the first notes in her song of praise and thanksgiving to God for his mercy, for she cannot tune herself without his strength, nor can she "go to the assistance of another who is fallen." (170) Here the song is a polyphony of love for God with love for others as she sings that "our harmony is then in tune when we help ourselves within ourselves with You and help each other in You." (171)

Swelling with compassion, the song accompanies Jesus on the road to Calvary in the images of cleansing the flesh and binding herself to him with "the delicate chain of Your charity and love so that when I am tied and bound to You and see Your fallen children, I will be able to go down to take them in my arms and bring them to Your loving lap." (172)

As Jesus was tied to the cross and fell and as his flesh was cleansed in the Passion, we who are fallen in sin are cleansed by the bonds of charity that tie us to him. The blood of Jesus is the "precious bath of charity" and the eucharist is also a precious bath and the winepress of the blood:

> "The cluster of grapes that was put in the winepress of the cross for you is not so small but that in the love that poured out from Me to you would be left for you a delicate, abundant bath of mercy and charity in which you could return to My arms whenever you wished to wash yourselves of your stains." (173)

This winepress is always tuned, the Beata proclaims, as she deftly harmonizes the notes of her imagery. Then she places the instrument of herself in Jesus's hands and implores him to cleanse her chords with the cloth in which he clothed himself. She skillfully merges the images of music and clothing: the music is charity which issues from Jesus, first to the heavenly citizens who are clothed in charity and then "from them to other creatures." (174) Charity was the song of Mary Queen of Heaven and of the angelic messengers, and it was also the song of "Your most sacred hands and feet torn open for us" (175), their delicate song "Your most sacred blood, which invites us with its sweet melody to harmonize our souls with You so that You may tune us with Your blood and play and dwell in us." (175)

Returning to the image of the sinner in need of cleansing by blood, Sor María sings the last notes of her song as repentent before Jesus she asks his forgiveness: "Forgive me, for the disharmony of my soul made me come to You, and I no longer dare look at You so You will call me." (176) Thus the contemplation rejoices in God's infinite love with images of the instruments of music and the instruments of passion, which the Beata artfully elaborates into a beautifully harmonious composition.

In order to appreciate the power of this ecstatic contemplation, readers who are removed from Sor María by time, cultural differences and possibly a personal distaste for emotional religiosity must endeavor to place ourselves in the company of men and women for whom the Beata's bleeding body was an immediate presence. Some of them had seen her bleeding side and perhaps one among them had even handled the bloodied cloth extracted from her wound; everyone had heard of her stigmata and was familiar with stories of holy people whose bodies bled from the places where Jesus had suffered cruel torments. When Sor María cried out to the bleeding Jesus, it is conceivable that her companions felt their redeemer's pain in their own bodies because they saw and heard and touched it in this woman's body, from which issued not only the menstrual blood natural to her sex but also a flow of blood that originated in her profound identification with the Lord.

Sor María's body was itself a powerful witness to the Christian truth that Jesus had been crucified to atone for the iniquities of human beings. Her physical presence empowered these men and women to believe that they also might experience the intimacy with Jesus that St. Paul had expressed in the image of putting on the new person and be inspired to amend their lives in readiness for the spiritual transformation. The fullness of union would have to await eternal life, it is true— but for life here and now there was the example of this illiterate, rustic woman to enkindle their hope that they might experience so passionate a love within themselves that they would desire to undergo, and might undergo, the passion of the Lord in their own bodies.

Because the text that Sor María creates in ecstasy is the reality of God's love that she experienced in her body and also her love for God that she expressed through her body in ecstasies, penitence, devotion and good works, it is fitting that the medium of her art is her body. Furthermore, because God consummated his love for the world by having his Son become man and suffer in the flesh, it is fitting that she consummate her love for God in bodily suffering.

It is this text of love and bodily suffering that Sor María creates, and the principal metaphor that she employs to create the text is blood. Feminist criticism reminds us that blood is "one of the primary and most resonant metaphors provided by the female body" and that "cultural forms of creativity are often experienced as a painful wounding."[34] I would like to suggest that blood is the primary metaphor for Sor María in the creating of her text and that it is something more as well. Her bleeding is the process of creating and her blood is her art. For her bleeding creates the suffering-love which is the text. Thus bleeding/blood is both the metaphor and the reality in which the metaphor not only participates but also wholly becomes by dint of its participation. Or, to return to the language of the icon, the bleeding/blood and the body of Sor María are transformed from icon into the reality which the icon represents and from medium into the text itself—which text is the art of loving.

Even in the portion of the text that is not ecstatic, that is, the letter to the gentleman of Segovia, the language is distinctively Sor María's, metaphorical rather than argumentative, as she urges him to "retreat to that royal chamber of the merciful bosom of the Son of God." (181) Nor does she retreat from her body to lecture from a citadel of abstraction; her appeal remains bodily as she cries out: "See Him placed on that cruel, pitiful cross; embrace it with the arms of your pity if you wish to gird yourself against the fierce tempests that go about this sad land of our fierce exile." (181) She joins with Jesus to offer the gentleman a maternal embrace "in those arms of Jesus Who raised you up and redeemed you by His most sacred passion." (181)

Scholars of mystical literature habitually complain that the texts they labor to explicate exceed intellectual analysis, yet they accept the fact of inscrutability and go on with their work anyway. They manage to find bits and pieces of the text that submit to the rigors of conventional methodologies. As critics who treat mystical and ecstatic texts, we would do well to heed the counsel of religious phenomenologists and feminist scholars, both of whom are necessarily cautious about the effectiveness of conceptual approaches, although the reasons for their caution are different.

For religious phenomenologists it is plain enough that the subject of their inquiry cannot be circumscribed by language; no amount of conceptualizing will put God in a box. At the same time they do not reject out of hand the work of the intellect. They respect methodologies for the knowledge they yield, although the knowledge they recognize as true remains for them inadequate. It is commonly said in religious circles that language about God is only a finger pointing at the moon; so long as it points in the right direction, the finger draws attention to understandings that are true albeit inadequate.

The feminist scholar goes one step further. Not only does she have questions about how accurately the finger points but—and here let us see the moon as metaphor for the literary text—she wonders about the moon itself. She would have us look first of all to another moon—the woman's text—that by previous standards would not have made its way into the canon. Then she would ask us not to sight along our finger with the eye of the intellect but to leap for the moon with our entire body.[35]

It is this kind of leaping that we readers must make in the presence of Sor María's ecstatic text. In spite of individual sightings of the inner structure of the contemplations and their indebtedness to the context of literary models, the text remains a distant moon unless we somehow experience it with quickened senses and emotions and unless, like the men and women who were physically present at her drama, we engage the text in the fullness of our bodies and thus engage the woman, who in the fullness of her body, is the text.

Conclusion

"There is no middle ground between extremes," wrote the author of the summary of Sor María's life in *The Book of Prayer.* "Either these matters are the most perfect and holy we know in the world," he continued, "or the worst and most imperfect." (129) The statement is an accurate reflection of the attitude of the Beata's contemporaries, some of whom shared the author's view that she qualified for sainthood while others were equally passionate in their denunciations. The middle ground that eluded her contemporaries, who lacked the equanimity to assess objectively the conflicting points of view or whose expectations and proclivities predisposed them to favor or disfavor the Beata, may be discernible to modern scholarship which, even though it suffers its own deficiencies of judgment, ought not suffer the biases of Sor María's time.

Sor María's words as recorded in the defense and transcriptions of her text reveal a devout Catholic woman who had striven since childhood to imitate Jesus Christ and love God wholeheartedly. She tilled her inner garden diligently with ascetic practices and devotions that were consonant with Church teaching in order to realize with God's grace the harmony of wills that she believed every Christian should seek.

Had Sor María been of a different spiritual disposition and the religious climate other than it was, she might have lived out her ardent desire to experience God's intimate love in the safety of anonymity. But the Beata was zealous by temperament as well as by the example of her father, who was known as something of a religious fanatic, and by the tradition of excessive piety that marked Christianity from the early days of the desert anchorites. She was also naively trusting to have embraced men freely, permitted them to stay alone with her at night and obeyed her confessors in matters that opened her to gossip.

Though neither heretic nor harlot, the Beata might have been a victim of her own naivite, the turmoil of her times and the motives of other people. The motives of those who sought reform of the Dominican Order in the spirit of Savonarola are uncomplicated enough to detect. There is no need to ascribe questionable intentions like personal ambition to their actions in order to appreciate the Beata's precarious position as she became the oracle of their enterprise. It would have taken a remarkably strong-minded woman to have distanced herself from the reformers when she was their dependent in all ways and personally lived out the ideals that impelled them to reform.

The religious upheavals that characterized these years affected her standing not only with the Dominican Order but also in the larger arena of religious reform that the Church and state together sanctioned. In his effort to reform the Church as an institution and renew it spiritually, Cardinal Cisneros needed the rich assortment of talents that he found in the laity and religious. The Beata of Piedrahita was an especially important member of his spiritual army for her oracular voice informed the program with an authority that was no less than divine. But if Sor María was an instrument for change in a time of change, it was principally at the discretion of men like Cisneros who were in positions of power and whose work was in turn empowered by her prophecies.

That Sor María served the reform at the discretion of men is indicative of the status of women in Spanish society in the sixteenth century. Spain was no different from other European countries where the Church's ambiguous attitude toward women recognized little middle ground between saint and sinner; the female either ennobled the male or enslaved him in the flesh. Sor María was a victim of this ambiguous attitude, not in the sense that she was necessarily aware of being mistreated by men but that she and her society inherited views of women that affected how she perceived herself and others saw her.

Ambiguity cuts through much of the literature of the period. On the one hand, the emergent mysticism that was destined for splendor in the lives and writings of John of the Cross and Teresa of Ávila valued the experiential, and its exponents taught that the inner way was open to all, irrespective of social status, education or sex. Francisco de Osuna drew no lines in the matter of contemplation; unlike some theologians, he did not reserve the higher reaches of prayer for the religious elite who elected the monastery over marriage. "God does not discriminate," advises Osuna, and "this communion [with God] is just as available to you, whoever you are, as to other people, for you are no less made in the image of God than others."[1] Later, Fray Luis de Granada in his *Book of Prayer and Meditation* (1554) was equally insistent that the most inward, delicate prayer was accessible to all who desired to love God, while Teresa of Ávila claimed mental prayer and mystical spirituality for herself and other women.

In the early years of the century, when Sor María was active, the evidence is incontrovertible that women enjoyed respect and honor as models of spirituality. Not only did the writings of Catherine of Siena, Angela of Foligno and St. Matilde circulate freely in Spain but there was esteem for individual Spanish women as well. The Benedictine Mother Marta was in good standing with the king, Cardinal Cisneros and a large number of prelates who visited her for spiritual counsel,[2] and the orthodoxy of Mother Juana de la Cruz may have been suspect, but she was famous enough for the noted playwright, Tirso de Molina, to portray her as the heroine of a dramatic trilogy.

But for every voice raised on behalf of women as teachers of the inner way, how many others shouted their protest with the battle cry of "mugeres e idiotas" (women and idiots, meaning ignorant). The message was unmistakable. Women were not merely unprepared to teach, but by nature they were incapable of acquiring the learning that would qualify them to teach. Hostilities broke out as soon as a woman dared to teach, which is not to say that she presumed to occupy a university chair but that like Sor María she informally taught prayer and interpreted scripture. "In many denunciations one notes that it is not the error that concerns the learned man," one scholar writes, "but that it is taught by a woman."[3]

Typical of the anti-feminism in sixteenth-century Spain is the often-repeated phrase from the *Excellences of the Faith* (1537) to the effect that he, Fernando Valdés, the author of the treatise, is an enemy of the business of contemplation for "wives of carpenters." The Spanish version has a catchy ring to it that may have contributed to its popularity. The tone if not the wording of this passage was in the air:

> No matter how learned a woman may be, put a padlock of silence on her mouth in matters of the mysteries of faith and the Church. For it is certain what the ancients said, that the jewel which makes a woman prettiest is the padlock of silence on the doors of her lips for all conversation, and particularly for the mysteries of holiness and so she is not to be a teacher of the doctrines of the Sacred Scriptures.[4]

His condemnation continues:

> For fifty years in these kingdoms by the fame of holy women who performed miracles, how many have been deceived, the simple as well as the learned, clerics and religious, gentlemen and ladies! And by the fame of miracles many new styles have been sown against the life of the Redeemer and against his holy doctrine and teaching.[5]

Fernando Valdés credited the teaching of St. Paul as the source of his views:

> The literal meaning of these [the epistles of St. Paul], and even more so the spiritual meaning, is very difficult for learned men to understand; but even more so is it for the

> lady "beata" and the little woman who forgets about the distaff when she presumes to read St. Paul. Holy angels, consider what a tempest, what does a little woman, no matter how holy she may be, have to do with the epistle of St. Paul? And what can a religious or cleric understand about the readings of St. Paul if he attends school with little women except making new gods and goddesses at the expense of God and the truth of St. Paul?[6]

An atmosphere imbued with this anti-feminism could not fail to influence how men thought about women and women about themselves. Sor María must have been unsure within herself as a woman, an uneducated one at that, and consequently receptive to validation of her worth from without, especially when validation originated in men of rank, power and learning, such as Cardinal Cisneros.

Validation from without does not exclude the possibility that Sor María was assured of her worth from within. The example of women visionaries who preceded and followed the Beata indicates that their own ambiguity with respect to themselves was ultimately transcended if not resolved in the confirming power of God's love. Nonetheless, cultural biases cut deeply; even when a Teresa of Ávila was assured by the Lord of his steadfast guidance and although she acted resolutely on his directives, she was still a woman in the flesh who consequently was not altogether free of self-doubt.[7]

Given these biases, it is all the more remarkable that the Sor María who emerges from our narrative is a woman who was sufficiently sure of herself to undergo prolonged scrutiny at the hands of religious superiors. Appearance before the officials of the Inquisition was no light matter, even when political forces had conspired to ensure a sympathetic hearing. It does not require much effort of the imagination to appreciate the Beata's apprehension, if not bald fear, as she underwent the ordeal. If fires of adversity were required to test her spiritual honesty, she had them in abundance as the object of gossip, ridicule and formal denunciation. That she came through the fires at all is due in large measure to her conviction that she was God's instrument for reform and to the certitude in the hearts of others that her austerities, penances and ecstasies inspired. She may have benefited from the favor of politically influential men, but it is well to remember that it was she as a penitent, visionary and ecstatic woman who inspired their support in the first place.

The middle ground that the author of the "Summary" claimed was impossible to achieve in the matter of Sor María may not be a space between extremes waiting to be occupied or the as-yet-indiscernible reconciliation of opposing terms but rather the reality of ambiguity that is embedded deeply in the Christian experience. As such, the middle ground would not yield definible boundaries or disappear under the pressure of good intentions and rational discourse.

The reality of ambiguity is also embedded in the experience of women who live on the margins of societies that, like Spain in the sixteenth century, are governed by men according to values that validate their experience as men. As marginal creatures women are "neither inside nor outside, neither known nor unknown."[8] "It is this marginal position," this author notes, "that has enabled male culture sometimes to vilify women as representing darkness and chaos, to view them as Lilith or the Whore of Babylon, and sometimes to elevate them as the representatives of a higher and purer nature, to venerate them as Virgins and Mothers of God."[9]

This observation gives further meaning to the statement about Sor María that "there is no middle ground between extremes." But there is also the ambiguous ground of marginality that proved empowering for Sor María. Who would have listened to an uneducated, peasant woman under ordinary circumstances? But have her speak in ecstasy and her sex, rustic origins and lack of education are transformed into reasons to believe her and further magnify the Lord who has magnified her.

In weakness is strength; in disenfranchisement, power; in obscurity, renown; in ignorance, wisdom; in suffering, joy. Thus the ambiguity of the Christian experience as lived in the person of the crucified/resurrected Christ deepens with the ambiguity of the marginalized woman who was conscious of being crucified in her own body and who experienced in her lifetime a resurrection of sorts.

There is no need for ambiguity on the part of scholars and critics with respect to the importance of Sor María of Santo Domingo. She was a pivotal figure in her time as the catalyst and criterion of religious reform. Her writings are an invaluable resource for assessing theological developments in the early part of the century, especially the heretical teachings of the *alumbrados.* In her teaching and life she is a significant precursor of Teresa of Ávila who, although she does not mention the Beata and *The Book of Prayer,* probably knew about Sor María because both women were from the region of Ávila and also for the reason that Teresa's Dominican confessors were undoubtedly acquainted with the Beata through the oral tradition of the order as well as the contemporary chronicles that kept the story of the famous ecstatic alive. Whatever the extent of Teresa's familiarity with Sor María, the women are linked in the general sense that Teresa's caution about practicing mental prayer and teaching the inner way, which she herself traveled, was conditioned by the events of earlier decades when female visionaries tested the waters of spirituality and some, like the Beata, swam securely in orthodoxy, while *alumbradas* and others drifted into heresy.

In addition to these reasons for Sor María's significance is the importance of her *Book* as literature and the opportunity it provides to pursue questions about the meaning of "text." in terms of ecstatic writing and women's writing. Finally, the fact that the *Book* exists at all is remarkable. Buried for centuries in the archives, it is a rare find, especially for scholars intent on compiling a feminist canon. The voice of one woman, unlettered and of peasant stock, *The Book of Prayer* of Sor María of Santo Domingo is a small but firm insistence that the anonymity of women's past yield names and faces, hearts, minds. . . and soul.

Part II

The Book of Prayer of Sor María of Santo Domingo

The Prayer and Contemplation of the Very Devout Religious Woman and Great Handmaid of God, Sor María of the Order and Habit of Saint Dominic, Directed to the Most Reverend Lord, Cardinal and Bishop of Tortosa, Our Father, Inquisitor General, and my Lord.

To the Most Reverend Father and Lord in Christ, my Lord Don Adrian of Utrecht, by divine grace and mercy Cardinal Presbyter of St. John and St. Paul of the Holy Roman Church, Bishop of Tortosa, and Inquisitor General of Heretical Wickedness in the Kingdoms of Castile and Aragon, a priest (though unworthy) of your Grace, and your most certain and affectionate servant, sends greetings, reverence and filial obedience.[1]

ORacion y comtemplacion de la muy deuota religiosa y gran sierua de dios: soror maria de sancto do mingo de su ordẽ y habito: di- rigida al muy reuerendissi mo señor cardenal y obi spo de Tortosa nue- stro padre gen̄ral inq̄sidor ⁊ mi señor.

Prologue

In many and diverse ways, most reverend Lord, God reveals His love as intimately today as He did most piously in the time of His most sacramental passion, even though we are more sinful now than then. In our day He gives us a person who is reminiscent of the crucified person of Christ for the good and glory of virtuous people who always keep the Crucified Christ in their thoughts and the faithful Christians who follow and believe in Him as well as for the condemnation of the ungrateful, evil people who disregard Him and the unfaithful who doubt Him. I believe that your Grace will have heard about this handmaid of whom I intend to speak.

By the grace God has inspired in her, the Crucified Christ is never separated from her pure heart and chaste thoughts, not even for a single entire hour. Considering that all good comes to us from His passion and death and without it, all evil, she realizes that the most necessary and beneficial of all thoughts and acts of spiritual devotion—that which carries us to the highest reaches—is meditation on His passion and death. Proof of the truth that she always is near the Crucified Christ is the miracle that occurs each year on the day of the Passion when her right side opens, pouring forth blood from the same place where the lance wounded the side of Christ Our Savior and caused the blood to stream out. She suffers intense pain throughout all her limbs and parts of her body just as Christ did. I will not mention other great marvels that God has wrought and effects in her every day and in others through her.

So, my Lord, what are we to infer from what has been said and is to be said except that the shedding of this creature's blood is caused by our scorn and neglect of the shedding of the Creator's blood or perhaps by a vituperation in some secret place. The malicious accusations against her goodness, the new manner of persecution against her person, the diabolical mistrust of her good works are no more than lack of zealousness in one's faith. The example of her perfect life is reason for all people to feel shame and embarrassment. Because she is an unlettered village woman, her words of sublime, beneficial teaching throw men into much confusion and even more so learned men. Against the latter, let others say through her what St. Augustine said against himself through St. Anthony: "The unlettered rise up and grasp Heaven while we with our learning sink into Hell."[2] I maintain, your Grace, that the unlettered are those with acquired learning and that in terms of infused learning, the Holy Spirit bestowed as much on this His handmaid as on any other. I would like to say more but I do not wish to scandalize those who do not know her.

Therefore, my Lord, accept the little that I say as an indication of how much I feel for her but am unable to express because my spirit is dull and my talent coarse. May your Grace and all others forgive me if I live deceived in believing that this woman is the most enlightened, the one who speaks best and the greatest handmaid of God among women living today (although she confesses the opposite). It was not for the reason of what she said, which proceeds from her abundant humility, but for other good reasons which I do not mention that I have vacillated on several occasions, for I had thought about printing the present work many times before.

But since I read it and had read and reread it time and again, and then again many more times, it seemed to me so Catholic and in such close conformity with the doctrine of Christ that I formed my conscience on my doubt and rightly so. For if the fortunate and exceedingly patient Job, desiring to speak of the holy resurrection, wanted his words written down with a stylus of iron and sculpted in stone with letters of lead, what doubt was there that I should want and have printed all the good spoken about her with letters of ink on lowly paper? Certainly none. Previously I thought that it was tantamount to sacrilege and worse than cowardice to back out of an undertaking of such good appearance. Might I be reprimanded because I considered it so wrong, though it may be? My reply, which is subject to correction by your Grace, is that if you order me to pick up straw from the ground for the sake of health, I commit a mortal sin if I do not pick it up so that the ground is clear of the last bit of grain. Likewise, if it was an error to esteem it, there was no error in continuing it. There was added to this also the importuning of many people which I bear. Since importuning more often makes us yield to what we might like to refuse, it alone would be enough to alleviate much of my blame. Finally, my very great desire to obey and serve your Grace with a present of such quality as this one takes away the blame.

I could find no better person than you to give the present for you are eminently learned, universally knowledgeable and a religious, devoted servant of God. As a deeply spiritual son of His Church and Inquisitor General and Defender of His holy Catholic faith, may you order the work burned and me punished for having published it if it is not what I maintain and state publicly. If it is such as I state, I beseech your Grace to accept it in the spirit in which it is offered. As reward and prize for my service, I only desire (if you desire it) the favor you do me in desiring to accept it and as a learned, discreet Lord to amend what may be in error in it and as a Catholic Christian to bring favor to the divine.

Division of the Work

Although the work at hand is small, most reverend Lord, it is divided into four parts. Accordingly, the work contains four distinct parts that correspond to the four ways she speaks and teaches doctrine.

The first way is when she is enraptured in the presence of the most sacred sacrament and after she receives it; it is the most devout, spiritual thing to see and weep over that my eyes have ever seen. The first manner of speaking and teaching doctrine corresponds to the first part of the work where she says "Oh my God, Oh my God."

The second way is when she considers the greatness of God in some marvelous thing created by Him and focuses her thought and imagination so intently on it that she is enraptured in contemplation, saying words that are exceedingly lofty and worth remembering. The second part where she says "Oh sweet and good Jesus" corresponds subtly to this second manner.

The third way is when she is enraptured and the prior and theologians in attendance pose arguments against what she says. She listens, hears and responds perceptively and to their satisfaction. Other times they ask her about their doubts and whether the opinion of the doctors is true. She then replies if a response is beneficial and necessary for our spiritual well-being, but if the question is asked only out of curiosity, she usually remains silent unless the superior orders her to reply out of obedience. The third part where she says "For I was the Creator of all things" corresponds to this third manner.

The fourth way is when she is alone in her cell writing letters to the Pope, our Lord the King, the Cardinal of Spain, the Vicar General and Provincial of her Order, and frequently to numerous other people. She responds to the letters she receives from many people in a sweet, elegant and fruitful style. The fourth part where she says "Jesus Christ Crucified" corresponds to this fourth manner.

Since it would be too laborious and difficult to print everything that has been recorded of what she says, I thought it wise to content myself for now with this little bit, which represents only a very small portion of the total. So that the hungry soul may taste this new spiritual food that is prepared in four ways, there is at least a mouthful of each of them.

Summary of Her Virtuous and Perfect Life

with a reply to the maligning defamers and gossipers without reply

Speaking with fear and caution about the matters of the Madre Beata Sor María of Santo Domingo, I maintain that there is no middle ground between two extremes, for either these matters are the most perfect and holy that we know in the world or the worst and most imperfect. The first extreme is evident in two other matters, that is, her doctrine and her life. Of these, if we wish to consider her doctrine, my humble judgment is that it is very holy and beneficial. Her teaching is exceedingly beneficial because it has brought and continues to bring many sinners to realize their faults and set them on the road of penitence. Moreover, her teaching enflames those who are already somewhat enlightened to be even more fervent in their love for God and strengthens them to seek perfection and grow in penitence. This is all that she counsels and she neither deletes anything from our holy Catholic faith nor introduces anything worldly into it. Her teaching is very holy as we observe in her profuse, continual weeping, her steadfast prayer, devotion, contemplation and enlightenment about matters of God as well as her grace and eloquence in persuading, revealing and proclaiming these matters without ever having studied and finally her perseverance in living them in close conformity and agreement with the holy doctors.

If the enemy is permitted at times to have a hand in some of this, he always does it with imperfections and defects whereas she always does these things perfectly and increasingly.

The enemy gives them temporally and they do not last but she has them continually and without fail. The enemy gives them so that the fallen are never allowed to rise up and those who are up, he casts down. He causes confusion in one who receives them whereas she enlightens blind, obstinate sinners, moving them to contrition and penitence, and she brings greater understanding to those who are already enlightened. She even confuses and defeats the devil himself for, as it is well known, in the midst of the torments which the demons have often inflicted on her and still do, they leave her, saying that they will leave her in peace with all her companions and they will not get mixed up in taking advantage of sinners.

We see that this handmaid of God is very obedient to her prelates and confessors and always has been. Because she never followed her own will and opinion but rather the will of God that governs her or the will of the prelate or the confessor who direct and counsel her, we ought to believe in the greatness that has been attributed to her. Among many other things of the multitude that have already taken place are the many times when her side opened in the place where our Lord was wounded with the lance—many people have often seen the blood flowing; when she was freed from and victorious over numerous severe persecutions that she experienced and suffered; and certain other matters that I will not mention because they are not appropriate for all spirits and minds.

We see that most or all of her contemplations or raptures occur either soon before or after receiving the most sacred sacrament or when she is before it and in its presence. Because the sacrament is and was given for our sovereign good and help, it would be blasphemy to suspect that our good and protection might change into perdition and deception. Given the frequency and length of her raptures and the fact that they occur in public, it is also blasphemous to believe that this very truth might consent to be betrayed into a witness to lies and that it would thus occasion such grievous offense (for the sacrament is so powerful) to Him and such awful perdition for us, thus costing Him as much as we cost Him.

The enemy never had permission to approach the most sacred sacrament, and those who received it in a sinful state with the enemy were never anything but more confused and blind and swiftly punished. Not even when the enemy is permitted more latitude—as will happen when the anti-Christ comes—will he be able to approach the most sacred sacrament in his efforts to disturb the sacrament's help and consolation to the faithful. Rather he will persecute the priests so that they do not celebrate the Eucharist. Then, because the faithful will have no other consolation, they will have to receive and adore the most sacred sacrament in caves and mountains where masses will be said.

In light of these matters and many others about her holiness and the fruitfulness of her teaching which I do not mention, I could not betray myself, even though I am a sinner, by granting the devil the victory of conceding that he played any role whatsoever in her works or the early part of her life, the goodness of which has been proven by many witnesses in the proceedings that have already taken place against her. We know that although she is the daughter of poor folk, she is of means and pure of blood. Her father and mother were very devout and led very good lives. It has been proven from her father's deeds that he was truly a good servant of God. As a child she began to serve God in wondrous ways: she suffered acute hunger; she fasted frequently for long periods during which she ate nothing for months and subsisted on only roots and herbs for other months; she patiently and joyfully endured intense cold, poverty, austerities, scourges and very rigorous penitence; she also received grievous wounds, which are evidence of the devil's harsh torment of her, as well as intense pains and a host of ailments, sicknesses and beatings. During all this she has been and remains more than natural for she has always been cured and continues to be cured not with physics or natural medicine but by divine power. And she remains healthy and happy.

Even though she has been cruelly persecuted through all this, and still is, her life has gone from good to better. The more that people who are unworthy and do not deserve to follow her have tried to destroy, defame and intimidate her, the more God has increased and increases in her and her followers the quality, fervor and reverence of their love and holy fear. The more, also, does God increase the quantity and number of religious men and women and lay people favorable to religion who are inspired by her to renounce the world, draw near to her and follow her doctrine and example with holy desire, humility and austerity. We see in her company very religious people of holy desire and exemplary life and learning.

Her persecutions are akin to those suffered by Our Lord and other saints who followed Him. Her persecutors are also either of the lineage of Our Lord's or persons of scant prudence, devotion and humility or changeable people who are ruled by their passions. Thus it follows that either her affairs originate in God or God flees those who seek Him and seeks those who flee Him. Otherwise He deceives more and loves less those who love Him more and He enlightens more those who do less to be enlightened and are more despicable, which is quite impossible.

We know that people of this sort are doubtful about two matters, and rightly so, and that in all her persecutions they accuse her on three counts, and with truth. The first is that they doubt that she does not eat and that she lives without eating. They say that eating is so essential to human life that even the Divine Word who became incarnate ate in order to live in the natural mode, and they say other things along this line. Similarly, they maintain that the disciple or servant must not be greater than his lord and teacher.[3] Thus, if Jesus Christ Our Lord ate and drank, so also His glorious mother ate and drank as well as the holy apostles to whom Christ said, "Eat and drink whatever you find in the houses you enter." [Lk.10:7-9] Who, then, can exceed or even equal them?

Concerning the first matter we can reply thus. I agree that eating is essential to human life because of the natural heat that continually consumes the lymphatic fluid on which our being or not being depends. But because the divine power that ordained it to be so is supernatural and therefore not subject to nature's rules, it can ordain another form when, in whom and as it wishes. If He sometimes refused to employ this privilege for Himself, we reply in the following manner: for us to ascend to heaven and enjoy His Divinity, God came down to earth to assume our humanity and to undergo pain for our guilt, to die in order to kill death and to live so as to restore our lives. So He humbled Himself and considered it good to assume human nature for these mentioned effects. Taking our nature completely upon Himself, He manifested Himself as man and set an example.

He fasted forty days and forty nights, not eating anything, and then He was hungry. In the one instance He proved that He was God and in the other that He was a man who ate, drank and did the things of a man without which we cannot live naturally. Since eating is something which among other things effectively proves that His most Sacred Humanity truly resurrected (which many doubted), He also ate, drank, was touched and had contact with others. This handmaid of His has given such notorious evidence of her humanity that no one would doubt it even though she lived like an angel in all ways. Therefore, it proves nothing to argue that since Christ ate she also must eat.

A second rebuttal to the first doubt is that, even though the evangelist's saying may be true and indeed is true if it is considered and understood in light of the end and purpose of the very truth he proclaimed, nonetheless, for the purpose of the others the saying is as false as the falsehood itself of the one who alleges it. For if it were not so and if these spoke the truth, clearly it would follow that St. John the Baptist was greater than Jesus Christ because the Lord said so with His own mouth. John did not come eating or drinking and the Son of the Virgin came eating and drinking.[4]

Thus it would follow that the first hermit, St. Paul, St. Anthony, Sts. Macarius the Elder and Younger, St. Hilarion and Serapion[5] and many other saintly fathers were greater than the apostles because they endured a continual fasting that was uncommon among the holy apostles. If these gossipers and maligners were to reply that St. John the Baptist in the desert and the above-mentioned saintly fathers in Egypt did not completely fast by not eating but rather ate something even though they fasted at one time or another, well, what will they say about numerous others who went many days and years without drink or bodily sustenance at all? We will illustrate below how Sacred Scripture teaches this truth through stories of individuals in the Old Testament and further proves it in accounts of persons in the New Testament and of some even up to our day. The examples are related in order.

We read in Sacred Scripture about Moses who fasted without eating and drinking for forty days and forty nights. Certainly he did not do this on his own as Jesus Christ did; rather Moses sustained himself by the power that issued from the words of God with whom he spoke face to face just as a man usually speaks with a friend of his. By virtue of the food He ordered him to eat and on account of it, Elias endured another long time before reaching the mountain of Horeb, the mountain of the Lord.

Moreover, we read in the book that recounts the lives of the saintly fathers about a friar called by the name of John who was already advanced in days. His life, habits and abstinence are related by St. Apellen[6] in the same book where he describes how he went to the desert where he stayed three consecutive years beneath a large rock of a cliff and prayed so unceasingly that he never sat down or lay down. His only sleep was the dreaming that he snatched while kneeling on the ground. He ate nothing whatsoever except on Sundays when a priest of exemplary holines came to say mass for him and administer the holy sacrament, which for him was sacrament and his only nourishment. This is also true in the case of our sister. It pleases me to have said all this because it is supernatural, ordained and effected by divine will and disposition rather than by human power or any other natural force.

Similarly we read in the aforementioned book about St. Mary the Egyptian[7] who lived for seventeen years on just three pieces of bread that she bought for three coins when she left Jerusalem to go into the desert. For the remaining years—as many as forty-seven—she lived on only herbs, although another book states on good authority that she spent the time without eating anything at all.

Concerning St. Mary Magdalen, we read in her story that she lived for thirty years on a high cliff without eating. We read further about numerous other religious fathers and mothers who went to Egypt, Thebes and Mesopotamia where they subsisted on herbs, roots and water, which is little more than no food at all.

Much later there came St. Catherine of Siena who the more she was enflamed in love and fear for God and desire to serve, the less she desired to eat and the more she abstained from food until eventually she ate and drank nothing whatsoever for many years. The handmaid of whom we are speaking endeavors in all or most ways to imitate and follow the habit, life and penitence of St. Catherine insofar as she is able and God so desires.

Recently in our days, not many years ago, we know for certain from an authentic writing and witnesses who saw and spoke with him how the Swiss man known as Frater Nicholas, who was born very near Unterwalden (the main place of the thirteen principal places that the Swiss call the thirteen cantons or communities of the diocese of Constance), lived and did penance without eating for twenty years on an isolated mountain in that country.[8] The Holy Roman Church beatified him in the year 1509 for the many great miracles he has wrought and continues to do.

It would not be difficult to bring in many other examples but such prolixity might rouse anger. These suffice as examples to prove the point, and if they do not, then a martyrology or the entire litany would not be enough.

Now let us see if by chance these men and women were greater than the apostles because they fasted and if the best of them was perhaps greater than our glorious Lady, the Virgin Mary, who neither was in such a place nor kept such a fast, certainly not such a strenuous one. So let these know if they do not already know that holiness is not judged in terms of fasting but according to greater or lesser charity. I speak to those who do not understand this truth because the Lord (who is not deceived by gossiping maligners but recognizes them for what they are) replies in His holy gospel to those who do know the truth when He says concerning such persons that "He who has ears to hear, let him hear." [Mark 4:9] Again: "To whom shall I compare this generation of children who say to their companions when playing, 'We have piped and you did not dance; we have wailed and you did not weep.'" [Luke 7:31–32] And the same Incarnate Wisdom says a little further on what we said above: "John the Baptist came and he did not eat or drink, and they said that the devil possessed him. The Son of Man came eating and drinking and they said, 'This is a man who gulps and drinks wine, a friend of publicans and sinners.'" etc. [Luke 7:33–34] Understand these sayings and evaluate these measurements. This single saying of Christ Our Redeemer and Teacher and the above passages suffice to close the mouths of those who gossip maliciously and open the hearts of those who simply do not understand.

The second matter about which there are doubts is the miraculous opening of her side. Responding to this, I maintain that if we consider what I will say shortly we will find as much reason to believe as to doubt because, even though this miracle is great and mysterious, it is not absolutely new in the world. We know that St. Francis's side opened, as did the blessed St. Catherine's of Siena.

I say that this event is not new in general terms and that it is not completely new because it is only partially new with respect to the corresponding kind and quality. That is, in the former woman it was her left side whereas in the one today it is the right side, as it was for Christ whose side one of the soldiers pierced with his lance. We know this about preceding cases because we read and hear of them, but we know about the present case because we see and touch it. But let no devout person or anyone at all be upset or think that I assert this in an effort to make an odious comparison or to place ahead of the great saints in heaven this handmaid of God on earth who still can err and be right, be worthy and unworthy, stumble and fall without rising in battle, all the while the pilgrimage goes on with sighs, moans and weeping in this world, this valley of tears. Because of this danger our Lord warns us in Ecclesiasticus not to praise anyone before death, which means that we are to praise and magnify him after life.[9] Still it is piously presumed and believed that the Lord will bring to a glorious end one to whom He gave such good beginnings and who perseveres in such marvelous ways.

Therefore, Christians, on the one hand and the other—on the side of the former and of this handmaid—let us not be ungrateful to God for the favor we receive but give Him thanks, for thus He is pleased. And let us not analyze the cause and reason for His actions. His ways are immense, inscrutable and marvelous beyond telling. Thus Job did not understand, saying: "If God were to come to bestow prosperity on me, I would not see Him." [Job 9:11] That is, if it is for my good or bad I do not know. If He leaves me in tribulation and temptation, I will not understand for I do not know the purpose of it. If He suddenly asks, who will reply to Him or explain why such and such is done. For thus it is. So let us cease asking about and scrutinizing His hidden, divine judgments that are exceedingly great in virtue, inestimable and incomprehensible to human reason, and innumerable in number. We will understand these judgments when we know and judge ourselves to be insufficient for understanding them. Thus as we fall silent in amazement we will praise them more fully and eloquently. And if we are crazy enough to try to understand them then we will understand them even less.

Therefore, let our understanding hold them in very great reverence and admiration and with complete exercise of humility. And let us believe that, although everyone lives judged and ordained according to His eternal foreknowledge, nonetheless, for our help and benefit He wishes—if we wish—that all of us be saved. When we do not discover the reason and cause of it, let us not continue wanting to judge. If we do not wish to err then let us remain behind and say with St. Paul: "Oh the depths of the riches of knowledge and wisdom of God, how incomprehensible are your great judgments!" [Romans 11:33] Certainly His judgments are great, as said, and similarly great is our iniquity if we wish Him not to be infinite and powerful as He is so that He can abundantly and infinitely bestow or take away favors. In addition, it is a great iniquity to want to comprehend and confine in our feeble minds One whom heaven and earth cannot contain.

Thus many have rashly judged this handmaid of God and the miracles He works in her while many gossip secretly and others malign her everywhere, unceasingly and without restraint. As we explained already about the proceedings against her, she was accused in truth in only three matters: that she eats when she has gone for a long time without eating; that she puts on and wears clothes of worldly taste; that she rides a mule and amuses herself with worldly but decent pleasures and pastimes. These three things are so criminal that no one can sustain his weak flesh without eating, drinking and some amusement, yet when she does them it is said that they are criminal. But they are not a sin for her or for anyone, for her religion does not forbid them. Rather they are acts of perfection for her and for those who realize that the purpose of employing such things in a good or bad way is to set a beneficial example. As we men eat for reasons of hunger and sustenance, she hungers and is filled with God's love. For since she does not need nor does she take natural sustenance besides the food of His grace, she eats to receive the suffering and persecution for having eaten by throwing up when she does eat.

The first shows her charity because new, secret ways of suffering are found for love and reverence of Christ Our Lord and Teacher in imitation of His most holy and arduous life, though it can be imitated only from afar. The second shows her humility because she is persecuted when she receives food. Her humility is also evident in her clothing, for by her dress she causes others to think less of her than they would if they did not see that weakness. Also, by wearing such clothes she shows charity to those who give them to her and beg her to wear them so she will remember to plead for them before God. And if she is unable to walk about and amuse herself with these things and other honest pleasures, let those to whom this matter seems evil consider, if they might be spiritual, how even with all this she may be suffering because she descends from her spiritual conversation and how she may feel afflicted because she leaves the sublime and returns to the trivial.

Morever, if others who work just a little must rest frequently, she who labors and experiences pain so intensely needs a little rest as well. For even though her affairs are heavenly, her person is of the earth. The frequency with which she is enraptured in contemplation while engaged in these pastimes shows that her thoughts were not on worldly pleasures but on the pleasure of God and that while experiencing those pleasures she does not push God out of her mind. In this she demonstrates that we must never push away thoughts of God, not even during our pastimes, and that we must always flee the honor and praise of people.

It clearly appears that according to what has been stated she is a stronger, more beneficial example to those who know how to receive it by her perfection than if she did not eat or wore rags or lived rigorously enclosed with a hypocritical display of sadness. So that those who are scandalized by this business not be scandalized, let them consider then the torments and pains she endures every day and the hardships, necessities and labors which she has borne. They should not judge the one without the other or else they will not judge justly but rather on the basis of passions, like one who renders a judgment on the basis of information received from only one side and without hearing the other side. Finally, we are obliged to assume the best about our neighbors even if we are in doubt, for human law assumes as much while divine law ordains us to believe thus and to interpret doubtful cases in the best, most salutary light. Even as it may be more just to believe and interpret in this manner (even though we may not be obliged to do so), it certainly seems to be true, for when we believe it to be, we make it happen that God's great, marvelous works are manifest in her to the honor and good of her and of us. If the consideration is done with clear judgment and dispassionately and if we believe the opposite, then the opposite results.

Since God does not have less power but rather far more and greater power to do good than the devil has to do evil, I fail to know or understand how a Christian does not commit blasphemy if he attributes evil to God and good to the devil when he says that this is the deception of the devil rather than the grace of the Holy Spirit, which it is and must be believed to be for many obvious reasons. The evil enemy tends to treat a sinner well at times in this house on earth in order to mistreat him totally in his house for eternity. We know that while Sor María was secluded in her cell the enemy often dealt her painful physical wounds and even made blood flow from her nose and mouth, her eyes and ears, leaving her for dead. This the devil would not do if it were a deception.

Since we know from many examples and experiences that the deception he most often uses from among the thousand ways that he hurts and tricks is to enter through God's door in order to leave by his own, he succeeds with flattery and large offerings rather than blows and slaps. So we are to believe that by employing his customary astuteness the devil labored to deceive her, but with God's help he is deceived by her. Since the cause of the deception is to take vengeance on the body, the soul is not affected. But further on we will see that by her life and teachings this religious has made many good people better and converted many evil people and sinners to do penitence. Well, if this is deception, then we must say that the devil has been stupid because in gaining one soul he lost so many.

Since the result of calling him stupid is false (inasmuch as he is an angel and a wise old owl), so also is the cause of the deception false. Who will make sure and certain that those who obstinately insist on believing and speaking in this way are not deceived by the devil? For if they believe that this religious and handmaid of God by whom the enemy has been defeated so many times—she whose body lives and is sustained beyond all natural power and whose soul is always filled with spiritual joy and is unwaveringly serene—can be deceived by the devil, how much more can those who think ill of her be deceived! Clearly, in believing and speaking about these matters, nothing is more likely than that they have been deceived by the enemy who has been unable to deceive her and that the enemy has made them understand and believe that he has deceived her, and this is the real deception.

The argument they make about some women is so worthless that I pay no attention to it except in the case of one woman, which has been verified by authentic writing. She was deemed a saint but later it was found out and realized that her affairs were bad and ended badly because she had been deceived by the enemy. I say that this case does not matter because as a general rule the argument from the perspective of similarity cannot apply unless all the cases are similar in all respects. If this is not the situation and if there is a dissimilarity, then the argument does not hold. If all the qualities and conditions that concur in the one do not concur in the other, the argument is invalid. Even if the argument were valid in the event that they did concur, it would only be valid to doubt that she was that good and it would not be valid to say that she is bad because the former was bad.

Just because a person may be a heretic it does not follow that his friend or my neighbor is one or will become one, nor is the consequence of an habitual action necessarily good. One who can be pope does not necessarily become pope and a person who has the potential for being evil is not necessarily evil. Those who are not faultfinders[10] nor have cataracts on their eyes will thus recognize and see that these arguments are hardly satisfactory (though not sophist) because they bear no resemblance to the truth. They are, rather, simply soap bubbles full of malice and venemous poison. This is evident in what is said as well as what is not said. There were many women who did what this woman does, and less, and the Church approves of them and considers them saints because they truly are. Well, then, why do they not mention these women in order to prove that the one is good as they did other women to argue by inference that she is bad? One swallow does not make a summer. I can think of no other reason at all to seek occasion to separate oneself from a friend by wishing him ill and calling him mad, or what Seneca says, and forgive me for quoting him: "Some dogs naturally bark, but by custom rather than by truth." But if the Pharisees barked like them (not by truth but by custom) and bit Jesus Christ Our Lord and Teacher, whom they slanderously defamed and said that He performed His works by Beelzebub, etc.,[11] then what reason is there to marvel that they maliciously defame and lie about this handmaid of His and say the same thing, persecuting her for no real reason? None at all.

We see from experience that the good person has nothing more certain held over him than the persecution of the bad one, whereby his goodness and virtue is examined and proven like gold in the fire and silver with the hammer, which the more it is hammered, the more it shines and the more the silversmith grows weary. Just so, if the persecuted one falls silent and does not reply, the persecutors will tire and fall silent.

We know that this handmaid of God who possessed nothing of her own and had only what is given her without her asking or asking someone else to ask for her (because she hungers only for the health of souls) has established and nearly completed in a short time a very large house and costly monastery. She maintains just under two-hundred holy women whom she accepts and receives each day. She keeps them with much penitence and has them go without shoes and keeps them very happy, content and plump. Not counting the expense of caring for many other poor women and men, both children and old people, whom she makes study and whom she educates in religion, she spends a great deal on the religious and gives many alms publicly and secretly. Therefore, if we consider how much she spends and do not know its source, we have to believe that only God, who bestows so much treasure from heaven on her, gives her this abundance of the earth's treasure. So everything that everyone possesses is from God who grants many favors to the person He enlightens that she may dispense her alms from her holy provisions.

Therefore, although the affairs as well as the person of this handmaid of God have been impugned by many powerful people, they have been examined by sentence of apostolic judges (established for this purpose) and for the above reasons and others which I do not mention they have been proven and declared holy and good. So it appears that her teaching is most enlightened and beneficial and her life and works are holy. When we see these two such marvelous things, and they are, we realize that the matters of this handmaid of God are not reasonable or average but rather holy and perfect, as has been said. As such they can only come from God. Since they are His, the enemy cannot have much or little to do with them. So it appears that God grants the world a very great and new favor by giving us someone through whom we can be enlightened.

If we ever wish to humble ourselves, let us recognize our sins and be inspired and helped to do penitence and amend our ways. It is fitting, then, that in acknowledging ourselves as blind and sinful, we open our understanding with the key of humility so that the shadows of sin will depart and the light of God enter. For it is certain and proven (without fail) that those who humbly and with holy desire draw near to this handmaid of God soon recognize marvelous stirrings in themselves and the power to be contrite and repent their sins and do penitence and (if they persevere) receive advice each day on how to correct and improve their lives.

But if our pride does not desire reprehension and our evil, stubborn habits do not want to change; if we do not wish to hear or believe what is not pleasing, even though we see and need it, unless we see miracles wrought, like unfaithful people of little faith who are moved only by miracles; if we go about asking for even greater miracles than her holy life and teaching and works and the conversion and benefits she effects in sinners—and let us remember that in the holy apostles and servants of God their lives, teachings and works are no less marvelous than their miracles, for the conversion and resurrection of St. Paul's dead soul was no less miraculous than the resurrection of St. Lazarus's dead body—then we scorn the mercy that God grants and thus we must prepare for the punishments that surely will be ours by His justice. For no one can escape His powerful hand. We must be pardoned by His mercy and our penitence or condemned by His justice and our guilt.

Because it is equally wrong to silence the truth and to lie—and so we will not be accused of this fault before the Divine Goodness—it seemed to us that we had to respond by contradicting those who gossip about, defame and malign the singular mode of living of this religious and great handmaid of God. If the response turns out to be sufficient, it is through His abundant grace. If it seems that the response is not sufficient for them to desist from their false opinion and obstinacy, I beg with all courtesy that what Christ said to His disciples and to many others in His holy gospel will suffice: "Everything and anything that the Scribes and Pharisees tell you, honor and do. And what they do, do not desire to do." [Matt. 23:2–3]

I declare that we can deduce two noteworthy conclusions from the words of this text for the correction of everyone. The first is that with respect to God the important thing is not who or what speaks but what is said. The second is that if what he says is good and what he does is bad, then we are to take from the good he says and leave the bad he does. Adducing the passage for this purpose, I say that if this religious woman is as evil and such as they imagine and dream her to be, then let them leave the evil she does, and if they have ears to hear and understanding and will to understand, may they take the good she says, which is as follows.

To the Readers of the Present Work

We advise the reader of the following contemplation not to feel offended in your soul that a woman in ecstasy or rapture of the spirit uttered the words and sentences contained in this short compilation. Nor may your heart be disturbed if you encounter words expressing amorous passion spoken in the mystical sense. For the Holy Spirit breathes where it wishes. It is characteristic for the true, excellent contemplative who loves God with all her power to suffer necessarily in spirit and body the agitations that we see passionate people suffer who love according to the flesh. Even the excellent contemplatives employed this language of love and were wont to converse spiritually with God, using tender, delicate words. For this reason the blessed St. Dionysius states in *The Book of Divine Names*[12] that the glorious martyr St. Ignatius[12] often said: "My Love is the Crucified One." But because of our sins more people nowadays are wounded by arrows of earthly love than holy, divine love. The palate cannot judge accurately the flavor of a good it has never tasted. Therefore, only those who already may feel their spirit separated from the affections of the world and joined to God in true love and holy fear will be able to appreciate and judge from reading this little work.

Contemplation While Enraptured on Easter Sunday

The Prayer and Contemplation that follows is part of what could be grasped of the words uttered by the handmaid of God, Sor María of Santo Domingo, a devout woman of the Third Order of the Blessed St. Dominic, while she was enraptured at communion on Easter Sunday, the day of the Resurrection of the Lord, in the monastery of Santa Cruz de la Magdalena in Aldea Nueva. Present were some religious, a gentleman from Talavera, a legal judge from the Chancery of Valladolid, a canon of Zaragoza, another from Segovia, and other ecclesiastical and secular people.[14]

Oh, my God. Oh, my God. Oh, my God. Oh, woe is me. Oh, woe is me who is not resurrected with You. When will I be resurrected in Your love and fear? When is the day of utter love and delight when I will rejoice with You? The day when heaven and earth rejoiced. Oh, my God, how alone and unhappy my soul who comes to You! How I never learned to awaken and be something for You! Oh, Mother of God, remember me on the day your pain was satisfied, on the day you saw your delight and happiness and your church raised up. Oh, merciful Magdalen, consider that you were like an orphan and stranger; receive me, a sinner, into the company of your Teacher and do not abandon me for having made myself an orphan and stranger from Him.

May I be brought to Him and received by Him through you. When will I see myself so happy with Him that nothing at all may sadden me? When will I be received in your arms so that my soul may be quieted with Him and gladdened by

Him? My God and my Savior, when will I rest sad in Your sweet arms? When will my soul be inebriated in Your love and unable to leave You? Since my will's disorders, which separate me from You, want to separate my soul from You, when will my soul cry out and call to You that they do not separate her from You? Oh, my soul, when my passions cry out to you in order to kill you, why do you not go to your God and let yourself be grasped? Why do you not complain to Him about the company of yours? Consider that the crude body they gave you as your slave is now your lord and has you enslaved. In order to conquer and avenge yourself of it, when will you embrace with the cross the One who resurrects by opening up the road I closed? I closed it, my God, with my sins and disobedience; Your delicate flesh, Your delicate limbs all bruised and broken, they opened it up. Your will and the power of Your merciful love opened it with them.

Oh, my God, when I fail to approach You and when I cast You aside, punish and whip me so that You will not demand the final account. If I often stumble and You do not whip me to get me up, then later I will be unable to rise except with much pain even though You may lash me very hard. Then scourge me there so I will not wait to give You the final account. If I stumble and suffer without You, the sad account will be rendered which for me is to remain separated from You and then on judgment day I will have no other account to render. My account will be rendered, and it will show me that Your angelic face has turned terrible. It will terrify the sinner because the ferocity which the sinner harbored within will make You terrifying to him.

Oh, my Goodness, even if I am completely covered with sins, You ought to show mercy and raise me up. You ought to loathe them and trample them and favor me in Your love and burn me in it so that by Your love and fervor and by my considering their abundance, there may be enclosed in me greater vigilance and desire to loathe and conquer them. So give me some of the love and fervor You granted Your devout Magdalen. Grant me this from the stream of tears that did not subside in her but dried up in me. And when will I go out with her in the midst of shadows to seek light and not want to return to my secret place until I bear Your light within so that I may come to You happy and sweet? When will I set my eyes on the four beautiful gems that adorn Your precious crown with which You rise up? When will I see You raised up to strengthen the weak and restore the maimed and sick to health?

Woe to me, asleep in the night and lacking the vigilance to go out gaily and happily to gaze on You in the still, beautiful morning. I have left the travails of the body and care of my soul, but the death of my soul, no, and for that reason I have completely forgotten You. Woe to me, who in childhood yearned to rise up with You but now, grown old in sin, does not wish to rise up even though You help me. Where, then, ought my desire be if not with You, my God, who is desirous of those You purchased? You wish nothing except that we draw near to You so that You may give to us and we may beg from You. You have need of us for our own need, which is Yours, and the need is not Yours but ours who are Your price. Your need thus is to meet and help that need we all have which is need of You. That need You have of no one.

Woe to him who does not serve You so that You may help him. Sad is he who in serving You thinks that he really serves You in some way when he should realize that You do him a great benefit in letting him serve You, for You thus help him meet the need he has of You. My God, I place my hope in You that You will awaken me in the beautiful thicket. Remember me on such a happy day so I will not separate myself from Your cross. Oh what a happy day for those who desire You and, considering who You are, embrace the cross! My God and Savior of my soul, remember me and may I not be abandoned by You, receive me on the delectable day when You rose from the dream You slept, waking some, restoring health to others, empowering others and raising others up. On such a happy day, then, instill fervor in Christian people. Scourge them with an inner fervor so that they may look to You.

Remember that You came here for them. Do not forget the services of those who love You or desire to love You. Have mercy on some out of consideration for what others have done for You, and may some not be chastised for the sins of others. Consider what You are to all and do not consider me who does not know how to ask for anything and deserves nothing at all.

By the happiness that You gave Your merciful mother today and by the mercy that You showed Your disciples, I beg You to pity me and sorrow for me. Gladden me, my God, so I will not live sad nor distance myself from my glory and my salvation. Rather, gladden me in Your love and holy fear and with the prosperity of Your people who live praising You.

> Having said this, she said three times: I have been wont to sin against You, etc. And she received the most blessed sacrament. Afterward she said in her own person.

Oh most kind and sweet Mother of God and Mother of sinners! Oh devout Mother who wished to be Mother to sinners, Mother of torments and pleasure, Mother of pain, Mother of repose, Mother of repose for those in pain and Mother of pain for Him who was all repose, you who were Mother of pain for Him! When He was in pain on the cross and cruelly tormented, He refused to call you mother, for had He called you mother then, seeing you sorely wounded and leaving you thus, the pain would have been more intense for you and for Him. He did not wish more pain in order to suffer more, but if it seemed to onlookers that He suffered more and your pain was harsher, the purpose was to avenge headstrong people more strongly. Therefore, He wanted to call you "woman" in the presence of everyone because He did not wish to feel maternal love, which was not fitting a hardened people. He thus deprived you of maternal love because that tenderness of motherly love was improper in One who was the Son of God and He did not wish to wound you further in this tenderness. So you who were a mother of pain for yourself and for Him by being a mother of rest for sinners, look after us now.

Oh sweet and fragrant lily, He wished to open your precious heart and He enclosed Himself therein by enjoying the clear sun of mercy in the fresh morning and imparting a most gentle fragrance of Himself to you. Sweet Jesus withdrew into you so as to draw us to Himself with the sweet fragrance that emanates from you. So draw us near to Him through yourself and do not abandon us.

Oh sweet Mother of God, what do you see in these books? Since all the books say that He will rise up, cease weeping now. Ah, how lovingly, softly and meekly she weeps, as if she were not weeping. Yet she weeps so grievously that the tears of her eyes dampen her clothing. Do not tire yourself further for they all say the same thing—that He will rise up—and one of them will say when. So consider all of them carefully and do not fatigue yourself weeping so grievously.

Oh devout Queen, give me some little bits of the pain and love with which to weep. Grant me this so my eyes will not tire. Woe is me for they have dried up and my fountains have ceased flowing. I no longer know how to call out to Him. And why are you looking at this little verse so much? *Exurge gloria mea exurgam diluculo.* [Rise up, my glory, I will rise up at dawn.] You are looking at what you seek. You find it and now you are sad. Consider it well, be happy, and do not be sad, for that great prophet wrote: "See how she goes to the little window to see if the beautiful fresh morning comes."[15] She looks again at her clothes and robes bloodied with the most sacred blood of her Beloved when He came through Jerusalem with the cross and when she, like an enraged lioness, ran to embrace Him in great agony. And at the foot of the cross as she sees the blood drained out of Him and finds nothing, she begins to say with both happiness and sorrow:

"Now my Beloved has taken away what He gave me in His sorrow. Now He, my Beloved, ought to come."

And she said, crying: "My Beloved, by whom are You more beloved than by me?"

Now see the one who gave You birth. Now see the living mother who saw her son die. See with what love and tears she washes and sweeps the cell while waiting for her Beloved.

"Lady, you see here this One who never knew anything but to bring you happy news although He brought you pain with pleasure in the first news, for He showed you what He had to suffer for all with respect to what He, who came to be enclosed within you, would take from you. Since this suffering is joined with our redemption, rejoice in what He says to you. Why did He want to send you a messenger of His coming if it was not so that you would not be frightened by excessive pain when He took away so swiftly the great pleasure of seeing Him?"

See our great King and Lord, and consider her words:

"My Love and my Lord, this is the One I saw on Friday in the hands of the executioners. This is He whom I found humbled with the cross and whom they tore from my hands. This is my Beloved who in His pain accepted my poor cloth and wished nothing more for I had nothing more to give Him. My Beloved, who put these lovely roses in Your sacred hands? Who put such fragrant lilies in such beautiful places? You took them for You were delectable, beautiful, white and colored to sinners to whom You showed yourself gentle, though injured to me. You took them in order to rejoice, gladden and heal sinners with them. Woe to you, Jerusalem, how you cast out my glory from you, not wanting to suffer their killing Him within you."

"My Lady, why do you not rejoice? Why do you allow your Beloved to kneel before you now that He has risen and is Lord?"

"Oh merciful God, how You wipe away Your mother's tears with Your hands!"

And He is before her, He Himself adoring Himself in her. He reveals what He placed in her from the Father and Himself by virtue of her faith in Him. He says to her lovingly:

"Oh My sweet mother, you see Me here now risen. Rejoice with Me and in Me for the redemption, which is now accomplished. Behold here your sweet husband, My mentor. Behold here these others who loved Me and loved you."

"Behold my Beloved who died for me and the one who pleased You so much with that little verse."

"Now I am risen and you will see Me suffer no more. Rejoice and do not weep."

Behold how joyfully she weeps, saying:

"Until now, Lord, I wept for Your suffering. Now I shall weep for I shall remain like a stranger without You, surrounded by sorrows. You will leave me and go away. With You go all those who lived in close conformity with You. You are to leave me without You and without them. But I beg You for the love You showed me on the cross and for my suffering there with You and for You, I beg You to visit those children of Yours who are left without a master that they will have one some day. Oh my Lord and my Goodness, have pity on me as You pity them. Behold the sorrow with which they returned in desperation to the table where they ate with You. Crying and moaning, they struck their faces. Your beloved one, he who denied You, stretched out in the midst of them all, not daring to rise for he thought that You hated him and he feared that the others would loathe him as well. And behold Your beloved disciple, telling them how You suffered all night and day, weeping unceasingly with them and me, becoming disconsolate so as to console me. May such love without faith startle You, may such strong love without faith astound You, and may You help them who love You."

"If You wish me to be a mother to sinners, help me help them. May your Benignity have compassion on them. Oh my Goodness, if You only saw (though of course You saw everything) how they all wept with me for You and for what I suffered when they looked at me! Ah, if You had only seen Your beloved woman looking for precious things with which to anoint You! When I saw them with that love, albeit insufficient, I did not wish to say anything to her or the others to diminish the fervor with which they grieved for You. For even with that tender love without faith, they grieved so sorely that they and she made the citizens feel sorry for their sorrow. She and all the eleven spent the night weeping. What comfort were their tears for me when I saw them weep for You! With what love and sorrow did Your beloved woman speak as she prepared to anoint You: 'I did not expect to anoint my Beloved with tears. And where will I look for His body which is so precious and delicate to me? Woe to me, if they will just let me anoint Him!'"

And how they all cried with her for their Master, "Oh most sweet Jesus."

With what love He hears His devout, loving mother, and with what benignity He replies to her:

"Even though they abandoned Me, they cannot cease to be My sons, nor I their father. They abandoned Me because it was necessary for all creatures to reveal their weakness and thereby clarify that not one single creature existed who was not sick and in need of My cure. Sin corrupted all except the woman who was so close to Me. From her alone was sin entirely removed. Thus it was proper that she alone did not lose faith. Her alone I made capable of such greatness. Therefore, all who lived at that time lost faith and in her alone faith remained. If someone else was to remain faithful, it was reasonable that the person be one of My companions for whom My words were sufficient for them not to lose faith in Me and to provide the fervor to keep it—unless it was necessary, as indeed it was, for all of them to lose faith."

"For all the world was damaged by disobedience and stained by the sin which I removed. Thus at the moment I died (for then I overcame and conquered the force of sin living in creatures everywhere in the world), all creatures trembled, and, as if dead unto the death living in them, all fell to the ground, saying: 'Either the Son of God or something very close to Him is to die now'. Therefore, it was necesary that, bidding farewell to the old clothes in order to put on the new, everyone would manifest new feelings, for death snatched them all from sin. In each one the foundation of life was being laid by the desire to receive life from Me. Thus it was necessary for all to lose faith and for faith to remain only in the one who was so close to Me."

She asks in her own person: "Oh my God, why did You not leave faith at least in Your beloved disciple since You left him in Your place with the one who bore You? In giving him to her, You told him that he was her true son."

He replies: "That was the reason he was the last person on earth to lose faith. Rather than have her lose faith, all those who were there lost it. He who was the most distant in the world lost faith before My beloved disciple did, and he did not lose faith until he saw My head completely bowed down. Then he no longer had power or faith or feeling for anything at all; he was completely frightened and confused. Thus he wept with My mother, suffering acute pain with all creatures who then sorrowed for Me. Then the old clothing of sin was removed from everyone and the heavens opened for them."

Oh sweet and good Jesus, how devout the mother You chose appears to sinners she is among, and how closely united is she to You in secret. When all lost faith, she alone remained faithful. Since her pain united more intensely with Yours, and since it was more grievous than the pain of all others together, she alone was faithful. At the time of Your suffering and hers, her rejoicing increased so that her pain and her joy were as one. She felt pain because, when she longed to die of sorrow at Your pain but could not suffer in Your stead, she changed, and taking strength, she rejoiced at the thought that through Your suffering Your will was fulfilled and our redemption accomplished.

When she saw that You were truly dead (though You were no more dead than alive), she longed to die from her great sorrow. But she considered again Your will and the redemption of all and with an enormous effort she began to sorrow again at the thought of Your passion and death. For this reason, then, she longed that she alone would be the ark of Your treasure and that it would rest in her alone until You rose from the dead and distributed it. Since she alone was enclosed in Your bosom, as You were in hers, how could Your faith not remain only in her? How could such richness be in a creature filled with sin? What creature was there so raised up as she who would be capable of keeping faith as she did? Who would know how to eat food so delectable or wear clothing so beautiful if You had not cleansed him as You had cleansed her?

For everything was sick and not a single creature existed who was not corrupted by wretchedness. Therefore, it was necessary to shake the grain from the straw. It was necessary to scrape away and wash away the slime with sorrow, tears and lamentation. Among them, there were some who doubted

You. Had they not, they would not have lost their faith and forsaken You and been at Your side with the ones who put You to death. Had they not, they would not have gone along with them and thus denied You. It was worse than losing faith when they said that You could not do anything because You did not defend them.They had so little strength to suffer for You and with You.

So it was necessary to cleanse this slime and shake this straw from those whom You took with You while You slept. Therefore, when You arose and revered Yourself in Your mother, You also revered her for that which You took from her, and You revered Yourself in her for what she had from You. As someone says:

"Now, My sweet mother, taking this richness from you which you kept of Me, you and I will distribute it to the others. Now we will banish the weakness that remained in everyone with that which you kept. Since My passion amazed My followers, it is reasonable for them to be joyously amazed at Me. And I want them to be amazed. I want all of them to shake and sift the straw and to be content and fully satisfied with the wheat I wish to sow in My followers for their sake and the sake of others. My desire is that no one be discontent with the wheat except the person who might put on the old clothes and the old man again. But he cannot wear the old clothes again rather than the new garments that will be made in him unless he replace what I give him with clothes made up of weakness, timidity and straw."

Oh, sweet mother of God, stranger to self-love, friend to her own sorrow for the consolation of others! Oh, she who is cleansed of self-will! Oh, beautiful purity of self-love! How is it that you do not consider your own grief in the absence of your Beloved so He may go to console and reconcile others to Himself? And with what love you beg Him to visit His own. Oh beauty cleansed of self-interest and self-consolation for the consolation of others! Oh precious and true spiritual love completely cleansed, cleansed of straw, who loves God so purely that she loves Him only for who He is and loves everything only in Him and for Him! Oh what timidity of heart, for so many desire and seek contemplation with tears and moans only for their own consolation and self-love rather than simply to receive from God through His consolation the gift of being made more agreeable to Him and brought into closer conformity with Him so that they will know and be able to do His will, obey Him and thus fulfill the purpose for which He created them. Oh so few seek Him for this reason! Who does not seek Him out of self-interest and amusement? Woe is me, for I do not know how to value even this.

Whom do you seek, sister, with so many tears and moans, and why all this questioning of Him as if you would not recognize Him with the eyes of faith if you had seen Him and as if you would not recognize Him with whom you walked for seven months? See how she asks for Him without raising her eyes to Him. She did not look up because it was not fitting to raise her mortal eyes until the spiritual eyes of her soul awoke. Moreover, she did not look anyone in the face after she lost Him because she derived no pleasure in looking at anyone except Him and His disciples. It was also not proper for her to raise her eyes lest her confusion become worse because she had not known how to look at Him.

She says: "Oh friend, tell me if you know Him. When those young people up there saw me searching for Him like a furious lioness, they told me that I would not find Him here."

He says to her: "Why did they not console you when they saw His beauty up there and His graciousness without sin?"

She replies: "And how could they console Me since I was searching for the One who had created them? As I recalled His angelic face, nothing else could gladden my eyes. But tell me if you know of Him?"

He says: "How long have you been seeking Him?"

She replies, weeping: "Why do you keep talking so long with one who seeks Him so madly? Woe is me, how I left when the sun rose and the beautiful Sun of mine must already have risen when the other rose! I had wandered about all night weeping for Him. Now what more can I tell you? Tell me, then, if you know where He is."

He says: "Since you love Him so dearly, what would you give someone to give Him to you? How much do you love Him?"

She replies: "When I think of Him and then consider the heavens, they seem a trifle. All heaven and earth, then, are little to give for Him. But really all that I have to give for Him is nothing, and I have offered Him all that and with it, myself."

He says: "Which is more, to give everything or to give yourself to Me for Him?"

She replies, weeping: "Well, if I give myself, who can search for Him for me? Or how can I give myself for Him if I have already offered myself to Him and if I am already completely His?"

He says: "Oh, My daughter, you will love Me and I will love you. You will bear Me within yourself and I will bear you with Me."

Oh most benign God who loves nothing but the creature! You desire nothing more of her than that she surrender totally to Your cross and thus give You a place where You may enclose Yourself in her so she may bear You within herself and You may delight and adorn her with Yourself.

Behold the cry she utters as she casts herself completely at His feet! Behold Him telling her not to approach and how these words cause her more terror and suffering than what happened in the past!

Do not fret, sister. Consider that our Beloved does not reject you. But now, draw near so you may awaken more fully by gazing on Him. Since you want all of yourself to be for Him, rejoice with Him in that He wants you to want Him in this way. Consider that when you told Him that you kept yourself for Him and that what you possessed was for Him and His sake, He then showed Himself to you.

Oh sister, see how our Beloved comes with hoe in hand for us to till the soil! Behold the task He assigns us! However, when He looked at you so you would look at Him, He did not have the hoe because His love was enough to make you clear your garden of the little weeds that always take root in this corrupt soil of ours. What is the hoe He orders us to grasp? It is penitence by which we clear the garden of the good conscience. And the channel through which water enters this garden to make flowers beautiful and the grasses of virtues green, that channel is our will that is conformed to His will, held and closely attached to Him. It is, also, when the soil is well tilled and our passions are conquered that the purity of the precious hoe keeps watch and tills the garden of the quiet soul so that it is continually refreshed and watered with the Beloved's love and warmth.

Who, then, would not rejoice to have within a fresh, beautiful garden where his Beloved could relax and rest with him? But the garden cannot be watered except through the channel of the individual will that is in conformity with the will of the One who has the sweet water to refresh and gladden it. Who could have any will or desire other than that of his Lord and his God? If you offered yourself to Him, how dare you bring your will out of conformity with the will of Him to whom you owe obedience? Woe to us if we do not realize that our gardens are dry and overgrown with weeds! Why, then, do we not realize that we have but a single hour of life and if we leave untended the weeds within, they will sink their roots and habits of bad behavior so deeply we will not be able to pull them out later? We ought to ponder this carefully, for when our roots are deep, even if they are pulled out at times, there always remains a bit of them to take root again and they are very seldom completely eradicated. Moreover, weeds do not wither nor are they eaten by insects as quickly as good plants are. Let this observation shock us as well as the fact that if the Lord sees a weed when He enters His garden to gather and carry beautiful roses and flowers, He cuts it, throws it away, and does not care that it is lost.

So why will you not run to see that the One who loves you and whom you loved (though lukewarmly) refreshes and enjoys Himself in gardens that He finds tilled? He will not tend yours unless He sees you with the hoe of penitence to accomplish the cure of purity and vigilance. If this is not reason enough to set you running, then you should be shocked to see that you are worm-eaten and bound for perdition. Realize that if you do not take up the hoe to be cured and if you do not labor to allow yourself to labor and to bear fruit, the Lord of the garden will enter and will cut you off and cast you out, and He will not care if you get lost. He will let you sink roots in the confusion of your will, and He will not care if you go about separated from His will because you will be separated from Him for all time.

So who will not always be very careful and vigilant to have his garden well tilled and watered? And who with purity of conscience will not keep watch over the channel of the will that is closely conformed to God's will so the water of love and fervor will not be lacking in the soul's garden? He who desires this but is not concerned enough to labor to achieve it is like a miser who wants to give alms generously but does not want to stop misering, saying to himself: "Oh, if someone would only come to ask me for something!" And when the poor man does come to this door, the miser lazily gets up to greet him, then goes through the house busying himself in search for a crumb of bread. The poor man says to himself: "Either you will give up or I will take you such a trifle that you will grudgingly accept it." So he sends him away.

Thus does your God come to the door of your heart, summoning you with contrition and devotion. He wants you to give to Him so you will accept from Him; He wants you to call Him, follow and love Him so that He may enclose Himself within you and refresh you with Himself. But you bother yourself with something else, saying: "I will pray and do more devotions later."

You do not want to surrender to Him when He calls you, thinking you will draw devotion from your cold, worm-eaten flesh later. You are deceived. You wander around lost. What strength can you draw from yourself to draw near Him unless the strength comes to you from Him? How will strength come to you unless you desire to receive it when it comes and strive for it in your need?

Oh most benign Jesus, You took the hoe and gave it to us! Take care that the garden we are should be well tilled and cleared with the hoe. May the trees of life bear fruit with the Tree of Life who unceasingly bore sweet fruit for us and sour fruit for Himself, though the fruit was sweet when He labored in His mercy and love for our relief. So let us bear sweet fruit for Him even though it may taste bitter to us. If it is difficult for us to suffer grief and tribulation, may it be sweet and agreeable for us to suffer them for Him. Let us desire what He desires. Let us embrace what is in conformity with what He teaches and commands. For He does not wish of us what He wishes but rather what we are capable of; this He asks of us, not what He wishes. If He asked what He wished, we would have to be quickly stripped of all dross and rot so He might swiftly refresh and gladden us and do great things to us in Him. This He wishes of us, not according to the loving desire He has for us but according to what our weakness is capable of with His help. He looks at us desiring this greatness for us, helping us gain it, abandoning us without it if we reject His help, for He wishes to raise us up to Him by our will rather than His power.

If we do not cleanse ourselves of self-will, following and gazing only at Him, He will not place His will in us; for You, my God, do not intend to place Your treasure in the midst of our rottenness. If we so love the world, You will leave us in the world until we receive fr om You the desire You instill in us not to desire the world, whereupon we will desire to leave the world. If we so love passions, You will let us have them in abundance. If we do not want to leave them, You will give them to us abundantly, which is hell itself filled with souls who love passions. But if we love You, that You will give us, which means that You give us Yourself and thereby transform us into one being with You.

Since a creature lacks the strength not to love what separates her from You unless You help her, and lacks the strength to love You without You and Your help, we ought to draw near to You and implore You always to inspire us to act in this way. Then, with the devotion and mercy You grant us, You help us resist the one and benefit from the other. We cannot receive such help if we cease imploring You with that help and implore You without it. Our Beloved revealed this truth when He did not allow you (Oh my precious Magdalen!) to draw close to Him but later He drew close to you; if you drew near to Him, you would not awaken, but when He drew near to you, He awakened you. Therefore, if one of you wishes to awaken, accept your grief happily so that He may call and console you.

Calling you, He draws you to Him to give you the power to conform your will to His. Your will is always conformed to His if you do not long for consolations or anything at all that is not in conformity with Him. When you realize His action in you, love the One who gave you such greatness, and may you know how to protect it. In your sorrows take comfort in that sweet mother who appealed to His will and who was unconcerned about her own consolation.

When you see yourself growing cool and separated from Him, run to seek Him in your heart with those two beloved ones of His. How fast the two ran, especially the Lord's beloved who ran even more quickly, neither believing you nor disbelieving completely. But he waited for the other, vacillating in his weakness and the bit of faith and love that remained in him. Although he arrived first, he refused to enter, saying to himself:

"It is fitting that he should enter first since I am the younger. If I approach and enter first, his grief and weariness will be greater, for he will say that, because he denied Him, he did not have as much strength to run and arrive with me."

Even after the other arrived, the Lord's beloved refused to tell him that he had waited to enter because he did not want to upset the grey-haired man. For that reason the other said to him after he arrived:

"Brother, why don't you approach?"

The other did not say anything to him except, "You draw near first, brother, for I am younger."

With the Lord's beloved behind him, the other began to enter, so fearfully and cautiously, and he cried out, saying:

"If He is there, what will I do? And if I don't find Him, then what will become of me?"

After approaching, admiring and looking at the place where He was, he said to the Lord's beloved:

"Brother, there's nothing here except the cloth."

With what agony and groaning the other entered, saying:

"But I left Him here. I placed His most sacred body here and left it. Then my lady departed and I went with her, my heart broken for Him. Later I returned and saw Him surrounded by his young men."

Behold the women running to them! How they cry out and act joyously, exclaiming that He is risen! Behold the men happy and sad, doubtful and yet not doubting! They rejoice because they wanted to, but then they become sad, saying:

"How will we assure the hard-headed ones that He is out of their hands? Since they are so obstinate, how will we be believed when we tell them that we are sure of it (because some women told us) unless we have firm proof?"

Behold the women departing and the two men, happy and sad, remaining at their departure. Behold the Lord saying to them:

"Behold your Master, sons. Behold your Beloved."

See the two of them prostrate, neither daring to rise. See the Lord say to His beloved: "Rise up, My son."

Crying, he says:

"How can this wretched one rise, the one whom You gave as a son to her who bore You? And I fell asleep in the dream of death. Woe to me, had I not denied You, had I gone with You, had I been near You later and gazed only at You! Have mercy on me, for though I denied You for Who You are, I did not deny You as my Lord. For even after You died, I could not leave You. So with Your love and the love I bore You (though it was indeed little) make up for this timidity and weakness of mine. Consider how You loved me though I knew not how to esteem You."

See how lovingly the Lord stretches out His hand and raises him up, saying:

"Son, how could you fall asleep at the time when the one whom I entrusted to you was left so alone? This love of Mine will ignore your error. Since they call you My beloved, so will you be to Me and I to you."

The other who was sighing and weeping said:

"Woe to me! If I heeded these words of Yours, I would realize that You are truth and could not fail us. Woe to the wretched one sitting at the table who does not think he will ever be without bread. Had I considered this when I was at Your table (where no one pursued me), a young girl would not have defeated me later. But she did not conquer me; rather it was my will which was corrupt. My disorder and timidity at not knowing how to regard You made me fall so hard. Woe to me! You can burn me in charity but You will not remove the pain I brought on myself. What a grievous injury I dealt You when I denied You in the moment they were scourging You! If I did not think about You, at least I ought to have considered Your honor. Where was my heart? Why did I completely forget all that I had seen in You and how much You had done for me? I abandoned everything and thus I deserve to be abandoned completely. Only the one who bore You took me to her bosom, saying: 'You have a Father whose heart is open to receive sinners and Who in kindness and mercy cannot deny you'."

"Thus do I approach You with the confidence she instilled in me and the hope in You which the One You are inspires in me. Punish me, then, and awaken me so that I may know how to esteem You, for I dare not count myself among Your disciples. Woe to me, for I still am ashamed among much younger men. What happened to me whose heart was so tender with love for You that I could not bear even to see You cry? And then when I saw you whipped so severely, I did not have the tenderness to feel it but denied You. I have committed such grievous sins that I will live forever humbled. I have committed such grievous sins that I ought not be scandalized at anything except myself and heaven because it suffers me. For the sake of Who You are, do not let heaven be scandalized at me and do not abandon or destroy me. Rather, perfect me so that I may labor in Your name to build love and awe of You through Your strength and my resurrection. May I not be scandalized except at myself, though not at my soul but rather the soul of my body. Or command the earth to swallow me up if You are served better by this."

Behold our Beloved has left him prostrate, complaining to Him about himself. Since there may be pity from one man to another among men but not from man to God, the Lord's beloved disciple took pity on his brother's pain. He cried for him and with him, saying to the Lord:

"Take pity on this one who is meek before You and sorrows so grievously. Consider that he is Your son and receive him as You received me whose shame and confusion are greater than his: I offended You more cruelly when I denied You because You entrusted to me the one who gave You birth."

Behold the two men weeping and our Beloved saying with deep love to St. Peter:

"Arise, my friend, arise, prostrate yourself no longer, no longer. May your sin not be placed in my penitence."

He said: "I dare not lift my eyes to look at You for I denied You."

The Lord says: "Rise up, rise up for the love I bear you and look at Me."

Behold him standing and having looked at the Lord, falling down as if dead and saying:

"I gazed upon my Glory and He gazed at me."

St. John raises him up again and the Lord said:

"Stand up, stand up and take heart from all and for all. By your wounds you will know how to cure the wounds of others. Take care of yourself but take even more care of Me than of yourself."

See how He speaks to them like a loving father and what strength He gives them. And where our Beloved goes there the others will be. Oh most gentle shepherd who goes about gathering his flock! Oh what a merciful shepherd, how He goes about healing the wounds that their sins (like ravenous wolves) inflicted on their souls! Like a loving doctor He brings tender ointments into their presence so that all may partake of the gentle nourishment.

Oh sister, why do you become sad among them since they all are rejoicing? Are you sad because they did not believe you? Consider, then, that even though they saw Him, they are not going to be believed. You rejoice in the consolation of what you saw (not remembering the proof that is necessary of how He was raised from the dead), and they rejoice with Him and the love they bear Him.

They long to prove to the others and satisfy them that He is the Son of God, and for that reason He is risen from the dead. Do not be sad because one of His own does not believe you for he will not believe the others. Thus it is necessary for Him to eat with them and to be touched by them so that evil people cannot tell the others that He appeared only to you who saw Him and that it was but an apparition. That is why He must be touched by them and why He must eat with them and deal with them, because eating and also having flesh is not proper for a ghost.

What proof would you have for these obstinate ones if they asked "How you knew" when you told them "He was risen" and you said: "We know because some women told us." Even though men and women are equal in spirit, in the eyes of humans man is stronger in the sense of nature. Therefore, in order to prove this to others and for them to dare die for it, stronger proof was needed than the statement of women that they had seen Him risen. Also, even when He was to ascend to His kingdom, He will not go secretly or in the sight of only a few people, for wickedness and hardness of the corruption of sin and disobedience are so enormous that they would say He remained there among men as something of little matter and because He was very tender toward them. Therefore, He will leave this earth with all certainty and at a great distance in the sight and presence of all, with His witnessing it and all of them watching Him.

So do not be sad that your brothers consider only their pleasure, as do you, but together with their pleasure they also think about being proven right concerning the secret of the truth so that they can affirm it boldly for the benefit of all and the greater shame and confusion of those who are stubborn. In order to confuse them, it is necessary to have well-certified proof in this matter that goes against their will and works so much to their harm.

Oh merciful Jesus, the thirty-two-and-one-half years—the time You lived among sinners, all of it a continual penitence—were not enough! The holiness of Your converse and Your marvelous works, Your suffering fatigues and torments for sinners, these were not enough for You to be acknowledged. Because they were so darkened with sin's corruption, it was not enough unless, after all this, You manifested such great things about Yourself at the time of Your departure. Even with all of the one and the other, the corruption of sin is such that this evil and callousness against You persists today among us.

Woe to him who is hardened in the habit of sin! How far he is from help, for his corrupt will does not permit him to see the truth and makes him loathe virtue. And to what coldness, confusion and callousness do the passions of such a person bring his soul, made so dead and deaf? Oh what a great thing it is for a sinner to burn in his God at least to be freed of passions! So love your God if only for this rest and freedom even though you might not have to love Him for His own sake. At least strengthen yourself for your own sake and develop later the strong habit of regarding Him virtuously so as to remain with Him by turning your eyes to love your God for Who He is. At least begin here so that the habit of rest and repose in virtue will endure in you. Whenever the confusion of passions, anxiety and disordered sadness combat and wear you down, embrace your Crucified Christ, moaning about your state and saying: "Lord, help me, for the thieves of my passions want to strip me of my happiness and repose. Lord, the thieves are stealing the beauty of my garden."

If passion defeats you, do no cease crying out to your Father. Though you may be destroyed, while you are sleeping and eating hold a mouthful in one hand and with the other shout out for Him to help you. For if you persevere He is not so deaf or without pity that He will not hear and help you. Be certain, however, that your garden is well kept, with the channel of your will entirely conformed to His, for the waters of help must course through it to water and refresh your garden.

Why are we given happy holidays if not to please heaven on earth and not to scandalize heaven? For you scandalize heaven when you offend the One Who is there. Oh poor and miserable sinner, who is not scandalized by the immense wisdom and power of his Lord! Where is your wisdom if you do not consider and fear this? May your wisdom be in loving Him. Apply your training for fulfilling your worldly obligaions to this task. If you are well bred and courteous with respect to what your God commanded you, then He will open your eyes to see Him and He will give you what you need to be agreeable and sweet to Him. Why not show your God the breeding and courtesy you show humans? By chance do you owe more to them than Him, or can He give or take away less from you than they? Oh wretch that you are because your perception and knowledge of others will accuse you of the neglect and bad breeding you have had for your God unless you approach and love Him. If you esteem and love Him, all the world will appear a trifle to you; everything will appear to be what it is not if you consider the One Who is. But woe to me, how dead I live if I think about this too little!

Most kind Father, grant me that wisdom and those tears You bestowed on Your precious Magdalen for whom heaven and earth seemed a little thing to give up for You. Remember me and have pity on my heart. And you, sweet, happy mother of God, do not forget sinners today, for we made you the mother of God. We sinners were the occasion for your becoming God's mother. He made you His mother and your will consented. Your goodness and your purity enticed Him to take you for His mother. He desired the enticement, for He fell in love with you; and He fell in love with you for what He had placed of Himself in you. That is why He fell in love with Himself so that by means of you He would be father to us and by means of Him you would be mother to us. So may you be the means of our help. And may you not abandon sinners.

Contemplation While Enraptured Hearing Music

Saturday afternoon, December 10, in Piedrahita, the day she heard a clavichord played and was enraptured,[16] and in the presence of the religious of the convent she said:

Oh sweet and good Jesus. Oh sweet and good Jesus. Who can know the disharmony of souls if not He Himself who in creating them knew how to tune them and knows how to play them? What sin put out of tune, Your blood tuned. For You know the harmony and disharmony of souls. You know how to harmonize and reveal in them the strings of virtues. But now if any musician does not wish to play an earthly instrument that is out of tune, how will You want to play the soul and dwell therein if it is not in harmony and tuned? For sin displeases You far more than does the untuned instrument displease the musician.

Oh good Jesus, hearing that playing, my heart became hard and my soul sad, for I realized that I was not in tune so that You might sweetly play me. The instrument of my soul was not tuned so that You could place Your gentle hand on the instrument of Your love, of Your will, with which You play the soul. I had not approached You so that the strings of my soul's virtues might be washed with Your most sacred blood, cleansing them of mud, dust and trash. Woe to me, sad and miserable one! Who can hear music without feeling sad or happy? For everyone of us ought to consider that she herself is a harmony made to be always in tune, agreeable and sweet to the One who created her. Thus she must feel sad seeing her soul out of tune, and thus she must rejoice when her Creator draws near to tune and cleanse the chords of her soul with the holy thoughts about Him that He places within her, or with the trials and tribulations whereby He cleanses and polishes her so that He can play her soul sweetly.

But woe to me, sad one, if I do not wish to cleanse my soul for Him when I call the One who is to play! If I shut the door to Him, clutching the disorders of my will, and if I prefer the death of sin and do not wish to enjoy my health, then how can the chords of my soul be in tune either with the gentleness of good thoughts or the severity and whip of tribulations? Woe to me, sad one, and how, my God, ought I to enjoy Your cleansing me and dusting my chords! I should have rejoiced and responded to You with a very sweet, soft sound, putting that holy thought to work and happily accepting tribulations so that my soul would be cleansed.

When the soft hand of Your love and fervor touches and enflames my soul, what harmony and knowledge of You and me You place in my understanding. Surely when I receive this and wish to conserve and guard it, I must give You immense joy and softness. It is not that anyone can give You more joy than what You have in Yourself for Yourself and for all, but still it pleased You to receive what You give me, not because I made You happy but because when I am happy in You, the happiness of You in me lives and is happy. For when we praise You, You do not rejoice for any reason except for the good that can come to us from You. With the understanding that is effected in us from praising You, Your most sacred and precious blood which You shed for us instills and diffuses its strength in the soul, whereby the soul lives and receives happiness from You. For if I do not receive the happiness that comes to me from You, if I do not love You, and if my harmony does not consist in understanding, then how sad must be my soul for You and me.

Truly we would never endure without loving and honoring You. If I am raised up, then I must go to the assistance of another who is fallen; and if I am fallen, then I ought to go to the other who is raised up in Your love and fervor so that he may teach and assist me. For our harmony is then in tune when we help ourselves within ourselves with You and help each other in You. This gentle, melodious harmony I leave for You and for all of us the happiness, gentleness and fervor with which Your most sacred blood was shed for us. Because Your blood not only puts everything in tune but also tunes and harmonizes once more that which is out of tune, its sweet harmony and strength remained in confession where it again tunes the melody that was out of tune.

That (Oh my God!) is why the one who offends You suffers such intense torment when he confesses his faults to You. Outside of the sacred sacrament the creature was wont to joke and talk about his sins to another person without any sense of sorrow or offense, but in confession he feels great torment when he confesses them to You. The only reason for this is that in confession the soul feels as if the mud, rust, stench and misery of sin that she embraced are removed. Therefore, she feels pain when she deals blows of repentence and moans that cure her there. Just as You were in pain when Your precious blood was shed to cleanse her, so does she feel there that movement by whose strength she is cleansed. Also, the adversary puts an obstacle there, which is a faulty sense of shame such that the sin is not confessed.

Thus these two, the most sacred blood and the adversary, fight over her, the latter trying to confuse her and the former to wash and cleanse her. The adversary burdens her with the weight of sin he placed upon her while the blood lightens it to loosen and remove it. When the soul has the rust removed, which was stuck and fixed to it, the soul feels the offense and sorrow. You do not give the soul this pain and affront but rather You strengthen her so that she tunes herself. But pain comes to her from the adversary in timidity and servile fear, and it is placed in her in a bad way that she may not be cleansed.

Oh my God, what instrument is as melodious and sweet as the soul that is tuned and in harmony? Surely none, for Your love informs her with a harmony and melody that is harmonized in You, and there comes forth from Your immense harmony a tempering and harmony on behalf of the soul's disharmony. Why, then, should we listen to such music if not to have our hearts draw near to You Who harmonizes the soul and quiets the one who puts us out of tune?

So awaken me who is dead that I may draw near to You with all things, for all of them and all artifices invited me to approach You. I hope in You that You will awaken me and You will. Tune my soul in such a manner that You will burn my bones in Your love and fervor. Cleanse my flesh and remove even the natural rottenness so that my soul is utterly clean and completely agreeable to You.

May my soul, my body and the flesh that is dead on my bones all serve You: my soul by loving and honoring You forever, my flesh by suffering for You, and with the flesh, my bones, all burning in the charity of the soul. And then in a short time I will seem to be always with my head reclined on Your lap.

But woe to me, for I do not know how to taste such delicate food. My good Jesus, I would go mad to realize that I can suffer for only one moment without You. So bind me to You so that I will not be separated from You. Bind me to You, my Love, and let the binding be the delicate chain of Your charity and love so that when I am tied and bound to You and see Your fallen children, I will be able to go down to take them in my arms and bring them to Your loving lap. My God, tie me to You like a crazy woman so that I may be mad in Your love. Tie me to You so that I may be tied and loosened, loosened to win for You and tied so as not to anger You. Our first father, Your son, was loose, not tied, and what he put out of tune as a consequence, in him and in us, You tuned with Your most sacred blood. You sweetly and happily shed it for all, harmonizing in its power all those who hoped in You and would follow You, covering all of us with a mantle of love drawn from Your heart.

You said to Yourself as You looked at us: "My blood will be shed for you so you may have a precious bath of charity in it and love in which to cleanse and wash yourselves. It is not that I am unable to rear you in grace and sustain you in grace without having to shed My blood, but it was necessary for your sake that I come down among you, become a man like you, and shed My blood for you so that My love (which I showed you by doing this) might raise you up more for Me and make you more conformed to Me and thus enhance your happiness with Me."

Oh good Jesus, Who for that reason left us Yourself in that most holy sacrament so that after having cleansed and washed us in it like a gracious vessel we might receive the delicate nourishment of life that You are. You left us another sacrament as a precious bath and winepress, commanding us, therefore, in Your own words:

"The cluster of grapes that was put in the winepress of the cross for you is not so small but that in the love that poured out from Me to you would be left for you a delicate, abundant bath of mercy and charity in which you could return to My arms whenever you wished to wash yourselves of your stains."

But woe to me who is sad, if the shame of my sins detains me, how will I go to You, my God and my Good? My shame is beneficial if I love You, but without Your love it is very sad and harmful and does not let me turn to You. So grave are the disservices I did You when I was disloyal and denied You that, even though You may turn me, who is as dead, to You in order to reconcile me to You, it will be more out of confusion than love. But since the winepress You left us always is in tune, though I may be out of tune, carry me to it so You may wash me. Do not cast me out.

May it be that whenever I hear something from which I can benefit, I do not reject it. For, my God, whenever I hear something from You, it seems that my flesh is tormented and my bones stir, and this I cannot endure. My God, the power of Your presence comes in Your words, and the confusion of my sin is disturbed as if You were before me. Even though my dead ears hear Your words—since the ears of my soul are closed and dead to understanding You and knowing myself—Your words disturb and then tire me. Since I am the instrument and You the craftsman who made me (You made me for You but no one made You nor did You make Yourself, for You are without beginning and end.), You tune me with the power of Your charity and love that I may turn to You.

But woe is me, for if I boasted of loving You in the delicacy of the day's first hour, I would see how I ought to love You delicately and in first place. If I had considered this first, I would temper myself for You with such harmony that I would cast all pretense of loving You far from myself and then, cleansing myself, I would make room for the living, secret power of Your love to be enclosed within me.

Oh good Jesus, how little I think about this. I place this sad instrument in Your hands for You to tune. Behold the cloth in which You clothed Yourself; cleanse me with it and do not abandon me. Oh sweet and good Jesus, and who learned and brought the music? Music was taken from Your city. Its sound came from Your citizens, from those nearest You, from those dressed in Your clothing, not that they have bodies or clothes but that their clothing is charity. They are clothed in charity just as they were reared and formed in charity. So music issued forth from them, a delicacy that issued forth from You into them and from them to other creatures. Even for this reason they say that the melody is most harmonious among them. Oh, what an angelic voice, and just as the things of Your city are sweet and beneficial to those who taste them and are not sweet to those whose taste is flawed, so music can be beneficial or harmful.

To one who keeps his eyes on You and his heart harmonized with You, it must be sweet hearing what issued from Your sweetness. Therefore, he will lift his heart higher to You with the music and delight even more in Your love. But the heart that may be flawed by disharmony and passions will not be raised to delight in You or abandon passions by the power of its melody and harmony. For if the sad heart does not have its eyes on You, then the harmony and delicacy of the music will cause both increased pleasure and harm to disharmony and passion. The reason is that the soul's disharmony results from the impassioned, disharmonized heart rather than the music's delicacy. Because such a heart does not taste this delicacy (although the ears may hear it because material, artificial harmony still does not fit in the disharmony of the soul with the delicacy and delight it feels in its disharmony and passions), it is enflamed even more with passions and is less vigilant and cautious about defeating and abandoning them.

Thus music must be employed very cautiously for it can be both very harmful and very beneficial. Who, my God , were those who taught music to the sons of men? They were Your angels—first, Your messenger who came to Your queen, our queen and lady, Your queen. She was not queen of You Who are king and lord of her and everyone, but she was Your queen in that she is a queen in Your love, and she is the queen, mother, and lady of all Your children. This was one messenger. The other was the one who conquered those who fell. That one, this one, and two others, all four were in harmony as one in whom there is no place at all for disharmony. They sang an exceedingly sweet song to console our father who stumbled, and two sons of his heard the song along with him. When he heard it, he began to cry, like one who wakes up, and said with great happiness: "If I am to delight in this, much more is the good that is kept for me than what I lost. So my penitence must be rigorous and I must fortify myself to do it."

Then two of the four who heard the music took it from the others. For that reason music is a delicacy drawn from Your heart, issuing forth from those who were nearest to You and are one with You. Thus, these four, enflamed in Your love, cried out with such delicacy and harmony that the sinner was made strong. Later, at Your death, another four, this time Your most sacred hands and feet torn open for us, uttered devout, loving words to sinners that we should embrace You, take heart, and rejoice in You. The delicate song of these four is Your most sacred blood, which invites us with its sweet melody to harmonize our souls with You so that You may tune us with Your blood and play and dwell in us.

Thus, as the sinner when he heard that sweet song (after having been expelled from that delightful place) took heart with it to do penitence, just so after Your death on the cross (bitter for You, sweet for us) and Your most sacred heart was broken, many who had fallen down in faint when they saw Your heart break came to their senses, weeping and saying: "We should not let ourselves fall and be lost, for the fact that they pierce His heart after He is already dead is a sign that He suffers for us once again." They then took more courage; but it was not that greater strength came to them from You but rather that they regained strength from You by loving and desiring You as they saw this happen to You.

Oh good Jesus, how sweet is the music of Your pitiful sounds to the sinner. If one thinks a little about them, he may come to taste and feel some little bit of the delicacy and sweetness with which it awakens love to weep for Your wounds and not remove them from his thought. Why, then, will the sinner who has gained strength from You to rise up with You on the cross and who carries within himself music and harmony from You, why will he not continually have his chords harmonized and polished so that when You play in him, he will bear You in himself and rest in himself?

Oh good Jesus, I offer myself into Your hands with Your sons and daughters. Remember those whom I love in You and do not forget whom I ought to love. Remember Your daughters whom You drew near. Punish sin in me, and may purity come through them. Forgive me, for the disharmony of my soul made me come to You, and I no longer dare look at You so You will call me. For when I am placed in Your presence, those who may see me with You will think that I love You. Since I do not love You, it is greater shame for me that they deem me worth anything to You.

Contemplation on the Feast of the Discovery of the Cross

At communion on the Feast of the Discovery of the Cross she was asked if the word of the Lord had been revealed before now on the islands which Columbus recently discovered.[17] She replied in the person of the Lord, saying:

"As I was the Creator of all things, it was fitting that everything I created should hear the news of My coming and that they hear about the pain of My death, as all creatures did hear it. Although virtue was revealed to everyone, the news was heard as if in passing in some places but was not received because not all creatures were capable of virtue everywhere."

At this she herself asked the Lord another question, saying:

"Well, if everything was Yours and You created everything, then, my sweet Father, why did You make it happen that Your word was revealed more in some places than others?"

She replied in the person of the Lord:

"I did ordain it to be revealed everywhere, but the evilness of sin which corrupts nature was stronger in some places than in others, with the result that the news would not be heard or received. In those places the creatures with the perversity of sin were like brutes and beasts in whom virtue finds no home. And although at some time in the beginning there were virtuous people there, afterward men of so many vices came that the frenzy of the many sins they committed blinded them so that they did not know if they were beasts or rational creatures."

"And all those adversaries that My beloved Anthony and other followers of Mine made flee from Egypt went there, and they [the adversaries] had such dealings with them that, even though they are open to knowledge, they do not exercise it. They sense the darkness and bitterness that covers their hearts and they rejoice when they hear something that can give them life with Me. But they do not have discernment because they do not sense it, nor do they call on Me but return instead to their darkness. Therefore, a great deal of time and effort is needed to bring them to Me, for the brutishness that remains in them is such that they do not know how to call Me for their sake or to offer Me that which I give them. Because of those that are not offered to Me, they neither offer Me the fruit I give them nor do they call on Me. They can do no more than act like brutish animals that are incapable of anything good whatsoever."

After this question she posed another, asking whether the religious who were there had made or would make any progress with those souls. And she replied in the person of the Lord, saying:

"If the fire is not lit or if it drifts to places where it is quickly extinguished, how can the rotten wood be lit that is mired in the slime of sin? First the fire must be lit where there is greater means and capacity for it so that where there is not such great means and capacity it may last and not die out so quickly. Therefore, when the marvelous flame of My love begins to shine in despoiled Spain, many other men of Mine will go forth who will not act like those who are there now. For these will act like brothers to those who are in that land, weeping, eating, speaking with them and describing such things as the heavenly city. And with the love they will show them and the beauty which they will see described, these men will win souls and bring them to Me."

Letter of Consolation for a Gentleman of Segovia in Reply to a Letter of His about the Unfortunate Death in Rome of García Valdés

Jesus Christ Crucified, our good, our treasure, our most satisfying rest for the laboring and afflicted, our most perfect consolation and refreshment for those who live with no consolation at all, and our most happy happiness for the sad who are anguished, afflicted, and in pain. In His immense and most excellent kindness He created us, and with amazing love and kindness He freed us by His most sacred passion from the most fierce prisons of self-love and misery. May He wish to grant you the peace, happiness and consolation which His Majesty may see befitting to your Catholic soul.

I received the letter you sent with such sweetness to me, miserable and sinful one. On hearing it read, I felt such sorrow gathering in my sad and naked heart that I could not express it, sorrow as much for the grief, sorrow and fatigue that burden your noble heart as for the disaster and death, so final and so unfortunate, of which you write. But I beg Jesus, our good, our help and our relief, that His eternal and immense kindness may gaze on you with the eyes of mercy with which He gazed from the cross upon His most merciful mother, our queen and mother. From His sweet, merciful and loving gaze springs relief for all our misfortune and sorrow.

Oh Jesus, our very merciful father! Oh Christ, Son of God! Have pity on those whom You rescued with such precious liquid. Have mercy and compassion on those whom You loved so dearly on that beautiful, merciful and blossoming cross, and with Your clear, shining light enlighten their blind blindness. Guide them, Lord, and show them the way so that such gracious emeralds and such beautiful diamonds will not lose the lustre of Your splendor, nor will such precious pearls perish that were bought for a priceless price. Oh my Lord, how immense is the mercy of our love, Jesus, and how great His love that He awakens some with the chastisement of others; that with blows to others He makes those careful who live without care of themselves; that with the falling of others He raises the fallen; that with the light of His mercy and the disasters and blindness of others He shows the way to the blind and those who have lost their way.

Look, Lord, this is not He but a voice that calls and cries out to us to abandon the One who gives such rewards to His servants in payment for their services; the One who does such favors for those who continually serve Him with such care and effort; the One who gives such good beginnings and dies with such horrifying endings.

Oh flattering and deceitful world, if only one knew your deceptions, only discovered such cruelties! Oh my God, why do those whom You raised up with so much love serve such a sad world where there is nothing good whatsoever, where there is only misery and unmerited, dolorous weeping? So let us consider then, sad, afflicted me, let us consider the entangled ties of this sad, deceitful world and its captivity; let us see how swiftly it makes us lose our way to that glorious, most precious city; and let us see how it blinds our eyes so we cannot enter into the knowledge of our misery, weakness and littleness nor enter the public squares of that great Jerusalem where Jesus, all our good and love, resides.

Therefore, my Lord, clasp the cross, so rich, strong and powerful, of Jesus Christ crucified. Hold tightly to the cross because it alone is our guardian, support and protection against the fierce dragons and basilisks that prowl about to devour us. The cross is our entire strength, our entire joy, that which consoles and accompanies our solitude, that which gives hope to those who live without it. With the cross our passions are conquered, with it victory over our adversaries is achieved, with it we walk securely wherever we go.

May your Catholic soul lift up your eyes to the One Who lifted you up. See Him placed on that cruel, pitiful cross; embrace it with the arms of your pity if you wish to gird yourself against the fierce tempests that go about this sad land of our fierce exile. Consider that no other safe port or any other anchor at all will hold us firmly and in certain security except Jesus Christ and His pitiful cross.

Cast yourself at the feet of the cross and cry out to your God to help and strengthen you, for so many souls are imperiled in the fiercely high seas of sin and iniquity. Though you bear a body draped in mourning, may you bear a heart free of anguish and passion. When you see Him very sorely afflicted, retreat to that royal chamber of the merciful bosom of the Son of God. There you will rest and kill the fury of this mortality and there you will find in your spirit the calm and repose that those who love God with all their hearts desire.

Endeavor without any cowardice to embrace Jesus Christ on the safest roads that the saints disclosed for us. For I assure you most surely that if the pearl[18] is healthy, the body will be healthy and good for serving its God, and our adversary will have to seek another road by which to disturb our good desires and thoughts.

I am exceedingly desirous to see you, and may it please Jesus that I might see you as swiftly as I wrote you. But that is not for me to do for now I am unable to do more. I offer you our sweet love in those arms of Jesus Who raised you up and redeemed you by His most sacred passion. May His Majesty dispose of your Catholic soul in such fashion that you always serve Him and never offend Him in any way.

Thanks Be To God

Seen by Saldaña
Inquisitor of Lesaragusti

Seen by Castillo
Vicar General

Notes

Introduction

1. Petrus Martyr de Angleria Eneco Lupo Mendotio Tendillas Comiti, *Opus epistolarum* (Compluti, 1530), included in Vicente Beltrán de Heredia, *Historia de la reforma de la provincia de España* (Roma, 1939), pp. 165–66.

2. Adelina Rucquoi, *Valladolid en la Edad Media,* II (Valladolid, 1987), p. 383. In a letter of February 12, 1988 to the author Adeline Rucquoi explained that *beatas* were similar to *emparedadas,* literally walled-in women, who in the same century adopted a style reminiscent of the earlier English anchoress. The *emparedadas* lived in a cell, room or house, usually near a parish church, sometimes a bridge or tower.

3. Jodi Bilinkoff, "The Holy Woman and the Urban Community. Sixteenth-century Ávila" in *Women and the Structure of Society, eds.* Barbara J. Harris and JoAnn K. McNamara (Durham, North Carolina: Duke University Press, 1984), p.77.

4. In his *Historia del Señorío de Valdecorneja en la parte referente a Piedrahita* (Ávila: Senén Martín, 1930) Jesús G. Lunas Almeida clarifies that in the part of Spain where Sor María lived tertiaries were called *beatas* rather than *monjas* or nuns. (p. 136)

5. "Pro tanto quod debemus pronuntiare et pronuntiamus quod eius vita et sanctimonia est commendanda et digna et laudanda, et quod dicta soror Maria debet moneri ut semper eius insistat, hucusque institit sermonis et beneplacitis domini et observantie preceptorum et mandatorum. . . . Ita persuademus et monemus quod similiter debemus sobsolvere et absolvimus dictam sororem Mariam ob omnibus contra eam oppositis, imponentes

supra illud perpetuum silentium omnibus et singulis personis et per hanc nostram sententiam ita pronuntiamus et declaramus in his scriptis et per illa. . . ." First published by Bernardino Llorca in his article, "La beata de Piedrahita, ¿fué o no fué alumbrada? *Manresa,* 16 (1944), p. 284. Reprinted by Llorca in *La inquisición española y los alumbrados (1509–1667)* (Salamanca: Universidad Pontífca, 1980), p. 271.

6. Petrus Martyr de Angleria marchioni Bellacensi, Antelato Murciensi in Heredia, *Historia,* p. 266.

7. Heredia, *Historia,* pp. 138–39. In the papers of the convent of Aldeanueva which are kept in the Archivo Histórico Nacional (Clero: Ávila, files 174–185) Sor María is mentioned as prioress until 1524. The story of Sor María was related through four versions: 1) Chronica brevis et generalis Ord. Praedicatorum II, written in 1524 by San Pablo de Sevilla; 2) Chronicon Fratrum Ord. Praed., 1510–1520, written by Antonio Senense around 1594; 3) a manuscript from the Archivo General de la Orden dating from the second half of the seventeenth century; 4) Chronica RR. Magistrorum Generalium Ord. Praedic.

8. For the account by Alvar Gómez de Castro see Heredia, *Historia,* pp. 266–68. Lorenzo Galíndez de Carvajal, *Crónicas de los Reyes de Castilla* (Madrid: Biblioteca de Autores Españoles, 1953), p. 563.

9. Henry Charles Lea, *Inquisition of Spain,* Vol. IV (New York: AMS Press, Inc., 1966), p. 6.

10. Lea, *Inquisition,* p. 7.

11. Marcelino Menéndez Pelayo, *Historia de los heterodoxos españoles* (México: Editorial Porrúa, S.A., 1982), p. 312.

12. Menéndez Pelayo, *Historia,* p. 312.

13. Manuel Serrano y Sanz, *Apuntes para una biblioteca de escritoras españolas,* II (Madrid: Biblioteca de autores españoles, 1975), p. 670.

14. Emilio Colunga, "Intelectualistas y místicos de la teología española en el siglo XVI", *Ciencia tomista,* IX (1914), p. 390. Although the Dominican Carranza de Miranda (1503–1576) came to occupy Spain's highest ecclesiastical office as archbishop of Toledo, he did not escape prosecution by the Inquisition for

teachings that were judged heretical for their Lutheran tendencies. He spent the last seventeen years of his life in prison.

15. Marcel Bataillon, *Erasmo y España* (México, Buenos Aires: Fondo de cultura económica, 1950).

16. For Francisca Hernández see especially Angela Selke de Sánchez, *El Santo Oficio de la Inquisición* (Madrid: Guadarrama, 1968). For María de Cazalla: Milagros Ortega-Costa, *Proceso de la inquisición contra María de Cazalla* (Madrid: Fundación Universitaria Española, 1978). For Isabel de la Cruz: John E. Longhurst, "La beata Isabel de la Cruz ante la Inquisición", *Cuadernos de Historia de España,* 25–26 (1957), pp. 279–303. For Pedro Ruiz de Alcaraz: Antonio Márquez, *Los alumbrados: Orígenes y filosofía(1525–1559),* (Madrid: Taurus Ediciones, S.A., 1980).

17. *Libro de la Oración de Sor María de Santo Domingo,* with a study by José Manuel Blecua (Madrid: Hauser y Menet, 1948).

18. Melequíades Andrés Martín, *La teología española en el siglo XVI,*II (Madrid: La editorial católica, S.A., 1976), p. 180. He says that the book was almost certainly published in Zaragoza between 1517 and 1522. It would have to have been published prior to the election to the papacy in 1522 of Cardinal Adrian to whom the book is dedicated.

Chapter One. Sor María: Her Life and Examination

1. Serrano y Sanz, *Apuntes,* p. 670; Heredia, *Historia,* p. 78; Blecua, "La figura de Sor María de Santo Domingo" in *Libro de la Oración.*

2. The first point in the defense of Antonio de la Peña published by Bernardino Llorca. The original of the process was in the library of the University of Deusto, Bilbao, until 1934. Beltrán de Heredia made a microfilm of the original in the 1930s which is kept in the Dominican house of San Esteban in Salamanca. The location of the original documents is unknown.

3. Heredia, *Historia,* p. 78.

4. Heredia, *Historia,* pp. 79–80.

5. Heredia, *Historia,* pp. 79–80, quotes from a witness who was favorable to the Beata. Blecua translates *confesos* as *conversos* in

"La figura." This account of Sor María's life depends heavily on Heredia's account in the chapter, "La pseudorreforma intentada por la Beata de Piedrahita y los procesos de esta religiosa", in the *Historia,* pp. 78–142.

6. In the *Anales breves de los Reyes Católicos,* Lorenzo Galíndez de Carvajal recounts that the Beata of Barco de Ávila was told by God to tell the king that he was not to die until he had won Jerusalem. (p. 563) In his *Archetypo de virtudes. . . Fr. Francisco Ximénez de Cisneros* (Palermo, 1653) Fr. Pedro de Quintanill, O.M. affirmed the existence of two beatas, one from Piedrahita, the other from Barco de Ávila, both connected with Cisneros and both saved from condemnation at the hands of the Inquisition.

7. Heredia, *Historia,* p. 79.

8. "Item, quoniam ex nimia communicatione et familiaritate quorumdam religiosorum cum nostra sorore Maria de Sancto Dominico multi saecularium et religiosorum utriusque sexus scandalizati sunt, et in diversas opiniones et iudicia devenerunt, quod non est sine magno detrimento et contemptu Provinciae et status nostri, super hoc, maturo cum multis prioribus in Diffinitorio consilio habito, mandamus omnibus fratribus nostrae Provinciae, tam praesidentibus quam subditis, in virtute Spiritus Sancti et sanctae obedientiae sub praecepto et sub poena excommunicationis latae sententiae quam in his scriptis ferimus, unica pro trina canonica monitione praemissa, quatenus dictam sororem nullus visitet, neque ad eam litteras mittat neque missas ab ea recipiat sine licentia R. P. N. Provincialis pro qualibet vice in particulari obtenta, etiamsi sit magister in theologia et praedictor generalis." Cited in Heredia, *Historia,* p. 85.

9. My account of the four examinations of Sor María are based on Heredia's *Historia* and Llorca's *La inquisición.*

10. Llorca, *La inquisición,* p. 47.

11. Heredia, *Historia,* p. 92.

12. Heredia, *Historia,* p. 97.

13. Llorca, *La Inquisición*, p. 48.

14. Heredia, *Historia,* pp. 100–01.

15. Heredia, *Historia,* p. 122.

16. Heredia notes that the words, cited in note 5, Introduction, are taken almost word-for-word from Antonio de la Peña's defense, presented the day before the pronouncement in favor of the Beata was given on March 23, 1510. See *Historia,* p. 122.

17. See note 5, Introduction.

18. Carta del General Tomás de Vío Cayetano al Capítulo provincial sobre el Provincialato y sobre la Beata de Piedrahita. Roma 29 de junio de 1508. In Heredia, *Historia,* pp. 237–38.

19. Heredia, *Historia,* p. 125.

20. "A pesar de todo," says Heredia in his *Historia,* "en la historia de la Orden esta mujer singular ha dejado grata y según algunos gratísima memoria." (p. 139)

Chapter Two. Portrait of a Beata

1. The material for this chapter is drawn primarily from the defense of Antonio de la Peña and testimony by witnesses which Heredia provides in his *Historia* and Lunas gives in his *Historia del Señorío de Valdecorneja.*

2. Lunas, *Historia,* p. 159.

3. See points ten through twenty-three of the defense.

4. Heredia, *Historia,* p. 107.

5. Lunas, *Historia,* p. 170.

6. According to Heredia in his *Historia,* Father Hurtado was "a person of great culture and extraordinary piety, and as a good son of the convent of Piedrahita he had always fought for rigor in observance, but according to the strictest discipline and submission to authority." (p. 107) Heredia considers Hurtado a reliable witness because he was not opposed to the reform that Sor María taught as were others who criticized; but Hurtado did question the spirit that guided her as well as her purity. (p. 108)

7. Heredia, *Historia,* p. 115.

8. Lunas, *Historia,* p. 176.

9. Lunas, *Historia,* pp. 203–04.

10. Heredia, *Historia,* pp. 104–05.

11. The implication of the Latin text is that just because a prophecy has not come true does not mean that it will not in the future: "Item, quia si aliqua dixit, quae non evenerunt, adhuc est tempus eveniendi nec ipsa tempus prefixit in quo evenirent."

12. Juan Hurtado, Damian de Ávila, and Juan de Septiembre as well as an unknown witness provide the testimony.

13. Damian de Ávila testified that he had heard Diego Magdaleno say that Diego de Vitoria told him that he had five or six pieces that were from the heart of the wounds. Juan Hurtado was doubtful about the prophecy that she was to give pieces from the heart of her wound for Diego de Vitoria to carry as relics to San Vicente in Ávila.

14. "Non obstat etiam aliqui testes videntur imputare dicte sorori Marie, quod ab aliquo tempore citra apportet seu apportare soleat vestes curiosas ultra decentiam sue regule. Item pileos in capite; item corallos in brachiis et collo et alia genera vestimentorum et calceamentorum, non ad convenientiam sue religionis."

15. ". . . item vestes superiores apportabat albas et nigras iuxta forman sue regule, sed subtus portabat certam faldetam gravem sibi datam a fratre Antonio de Peña, causa levioris oneris et elevatione dolorum cordis sui, quos ipsa patitur, cum propria debilitate suas non possit portare vestes ponderosas, et similiter proprios immensos et continuos dolores cordis sui ut letificet illud."

16. Lunas, *Historia,* pp. 189–90.

17. Diego de Vitoria and Diego de San Pedro testified to her mortifications, including fasting.

18. Heredia states in the *Historia* that whoever have seen how epileptic attacks and heart attacks leave the subject prostrate will realize that the Beata's symptoms are very similar and can be explained by physical rather than supernatural factors. (p. 115)

19. There are other colorful accounts in the study by Lunas; see especially her own descriptions on pp. 162–66.

20. "'Que rogando ella a Dios que la guardase del pecado de la carne, dijo Dios: no temas hjija, que yo te guardaré de ello. Interrogata si ella ha sido nunca tentada del diablo del pecado de la carne, dixit que no se acuerda que ella lo haya sentido'." (Heredia, *Historia,* p. 100)

21. Juan Hurtado testified that it was he who warned Vitoria against staying with the Beata at night. See Heredia, *Historia,* p. 108.

22. Among the witnesses identified by Heredia in the *Historia* are Juan de Sevilla, Juan de Azcona, Juan de Ceballos, Antonio de Benavente, Cristóbal Brochero and Sor María del Cordero.

23. Heredia states on p. 121 of the *Historia*: "En esto hay ciertamente un fondo de verdad que explica por qué, a pesar de los escándalos reales o imaginarios que aparecen relatados en el proceso, los jueces, no sólo aprobaron su proceder, sino que recomendaron su tenor de vida. Cierto que no consta que hubiesen apurado los medios para aclarar las cosas; pero en punto a inmoralidades debieron conocer pronto que en ello tenían mucha parte las habladurías y la imaginación."

Chapter Three. Reformers, Rebels and Sor María

1. Bataillon, *Erasmo y España,* I, p. 2.

2. "Grata est Deo et laudabilis cujuslibet status condecens observantia." Letter of December 15, 1495 cited by Bataillon, *Erasmo y Españo,* I, p. 4.

3. Bataillon, *Erasmo y España,* I, p. 6. The document, "Cédula de los Reyes Católicos sobre la devolución de los bienes enajenados por los claustrales," dated August 11, 1495, is included in Heredia's *Historia,* pp. 234–35. It reads in part:

> "Por parte del Vicario general de la observancia de la Orden de Predicadores y de los priores de los conventos de la dicha Congregación nos fué fecha relación diciendo, que muchos de los monesterios y conventos de la dicha Orden y observancia están muy defraudados por algunas ventas y arrendamientos fechos en el tiempo de la Claustra de las posesiones que los tales monesterios tenían y poseían y algunas personas habían dejado para sustentación de los religiosos de los dichos monasterios; en lo cual los dichos monasterios y conventos dellos tenían rescibido mucho agravio y daño."

4. Bataillon, *Erasmo y Españo,* I, p. 11.

5. Bataillon, *Erasmo y Españo,* I, p. 53.

6. Bataillon, *Erasmo y Españo,* I, p. 90.

7. José C. Nieto, *Juan de Valdés and the Origins of the Spanish and the Italian Reformation* (Genève: Droz, 1970), p. 89.

8. Andrés, *La teologia española,* p. 39.

9. Andrés, *La teologia española,* p. 39.

10. Andrés, *La teologia española,* p. 41.

11. Heredia, *Historia,* p. 256.

12. The source of information on the reform of the Dominican Order in Spain comes primarily from Heredia's *Historia.*

13. Heredia, *Historia,* p. 10.

14. S. Olmeda and Fray Juan de la Cruz are the two chroniclers whom Heredia quotes in the *Historia* (p. 54) as disapproving of Antonio de la Peña.

15. The document, cited by Heredia in the *Historia*, p. 71, reads in part:

> "El Rey. Por cuanto vos fray Diego Madaleno querriades venir a mí para algunas cosas complideras a nuestro servicio e a la pacificación e sosiego de vuestra Orden, e vos teméis que vos sea fecho algún mal e dampno por algunas personas, e porque yo so servido de vuestra venida, por ende por la presente vos seguro e prometo por mi fe y palabra real que en vuestra venida y estada y tornada no seréis preso ni detenido vos ni ninguno de los frailes e otras personas que con vos vinieren, ni vos será fecho ningund mal ni dampno en vuestras personas, sino que libremente vernéis y estaréis y volveréis sin que se vos ponga ningund impedimento."

16. Cited in full by Heredia in *Historia*, pp. 237–38.

17. Heredia, *Historia*, pp. 135–36.

18. Cited in full by Heredia in *Historia*, pp. 251–54.

19. Cited in full by Heredia in *Historia*, pp. 254–55.

20. Cited in full by Heredia in *Historia*, pp. 255–56.

21. Cited in full by Heredia in *Historia*, pp. 257–58.

22. Cited in full by Heredia in *Historia*, pp. 258–59.

23. Cited in full by Heredia in *Historia*, pp. 259–60.

24. Cited in full by Heredia in *Historia*, p. 260.

25. Cited in full by Heredia in *Historia*, p. 261.

26. Cited in full by Heredia in *Historia*, pp. 261–62.

27. Cited in full by Heredia in *Historia*, pp. 262–63.

28. Cited in full by Heredia in *Historia*, pp. 263–64.

29. Heredia says in the *Historia* that "Gracias a la condescendencia del General Cayetano y al buen tacto del provincial Loaisa, los de Piedrahita y de Aldeanueva volvieron a su obediencia, y ya no debieron dar más guerra, aunque con su actitud retardaron cerca de quince años la verdadera reforma y unión de la Provincia." (p. 135)

30. Heredia, *Historia*, p. 12.

31. This distinction is a pleasant resemblance to Teresa of Ávila's famous observation: "So they get it into their heads that it is *arrobamiento,* or rapture. But I call it *abobamiento,* foolishness." From the *Interior Castle,* translated by E. Allison Peers (Garden City, New York: Doubleday & Company, Inc., 1961), pp. 92–93.

32. Bataillon, *Erasmo y España*, I, p. 199.

33. Heredia states in the *Historia* that Antonio de la Peña "por encargo de Cisneros había traducido del latín la Vida de Santa Catalina de Sena escrita por el beato Raimundo de Capua." (p. 54)

34. Andrés, *La teología española,* p. 178.

35. Heredia states in the *Historia*: "A sor Maria se le podrá tachar pues de alucinada, de ilusa, de visionaria, de histérica, de padecer anomalías psíquicas y aun morales, porque rara será la mujer que encumbrada al grado de apoteosis en que ella se vió no sufra desvanecimiento, si una gracia especial no la sostiene." (p. 137).

36. Heredia, *Historia*, p. 130.

37. Heredia, *Historia*, p. 131.

38. Beltrán de Heredia in "La Beata de Piedrahita no fue alumbrada" in *Miscelánea Beltrán de Heredia,* III (Salamanca: Biblioteca de teólogos españoles, 1972) gives evidence on p. 449 for the connection between Antonio de la Peña and Savonarolaism. He cites J. Barrio in his *Historiadores del convento de San Esteban de Salamanca,* II (Salamanca, 1914) in support of the contention that Antonio de la Peña was the principal promoter of the translations which the group at Piedrahita offered to Cisneros for publication. See also: Marcel Bataillon, "Sur la diffusion des oeuvres de Savonarole en Espagne et en Portugal (1500–1560)," *Mélanges de philologie, d'histoire et de littérature offerts à Joseph Vianney* (Paris: Les Presses Françaises, 1934).

39. For a detailed discussion of these points see Jacques Lafaye, *Quetzalcóatl and Guadalupe,* tr. Benjamin Keen (Chicago and London: The University of Chicago Press, 1976).

40. José Manuel Blecua in "La figura de Sor María de Santo Domingo" and Heredia, "Las corrientes de espiritualidad entre los dominicos de Castilla durante la primera mitad del siglo XVI" in *Miscelánea Beltrán de Heredia,* pp. 520–31.

Chapter Four. Heresy: A Case of Mistaken Identity

1. Andrés, *La teología española,* p. 189.

2. The question received full attention in a polemic carried on by Beltrán de Heredia and Bernardino Llorca. See: Heredia, "La Beata de Piedrahita no fué alumbrada," *Ciencia Tomista,* 63 (1942), pp. 249–311, reprinted in *Miscelánea Beltrán de Heredia.,* pp. 447–461; Bernardino Llorca, "La beata de Piedrahita, ¿fué o no fué alumbrada?", *Manresa,* 1 (1942), pp. 46–62, 176–78; 16 (1944), pp. 275–85. In his *La inquisición española y los alumbrados (1509–1667)* published in 1980, Llorca returns to the question of whether or not the Beata was an *alumbrada.* His position is now much closer to that of Heredia, who maintained early on that she was not an *alumbrada.* Llorca concedes that she was not formally connected to the group of *alumbrados,* but her attitude was similar to that of the *alumbrados.* The series of articles is required reading for understanding this aspect of the Beata.

3. See also the other *Alphabets,* including the fourth, known as the *Ley de Amor,* and the *Gracioso Convite de las gracias del Sancto Sacramento del altar* and *Norte de los Estados.*

4. For an excellent introduction see Márquez, *Los alumbrados.*

5. Márquez, *Los alumbrados,* p. 108.

6. Márquez, *Los alumbrados,* p. 108.

7. Ralph J. Tapia, *The Alumbrados of Toledo: A Study in Sixteenth Century Spanish Spirituality* (Park Falls, Wisconsin: F. A. Weber and Sons, Inc., 1974), p. 31.

8. For an absorbing study of Francisca Hernández and Francisco Ortiz see Angela Selke de Sánchez, *El santo oficio.*

9. Longhurst, "La beata Isabel de la Cruz."

10. Ortega Costa, *Proceso de la Inquisición.*

11. "Que los cassados estando en el acto del matrimonio estaban más unidos a Dios que si estubiessen en oración." The version of the Edict of Toledo which I am using is reproduced in the appendix of *Los alumbrdos* by Márquez. See p. 229 for the author's explanation of the sources for his text.

12. Menéndez Pelayo, *Historia de los heterodoxos españoles,* p. 309.

13. Menéndez Pelayo, *Historia de los heterodoxos españoles,* p. 312.

14. The translation is from the text provided by Heredia in "La Beata de Piedrahita no fué alumbrada." His text are selections from the *Revelaciones de sor María de santo Domingo,* Ms. 82–2–246, in the Biblioteca Capitular y Colombina in Seville.

15. The fragment as translated does not include the small selection offered on pp. 00.

Chapter Five. The *Book of Prayer*

1. See note 1 to *The Book of Prayer* for information on Adrian.

2. See Rudolph M. Bell, *Holy Anorexia* (Chicago: The University of Chicago Press, 1985) and Caroline Walker Bynum, *Holy Feast and Holy Fast: The Religious Significance of Food to Medieval Women* (Berkley: University of California Press, 1987).

3. As Walker Bynum states in *Holy Feast and Holy Fast:* "And they [women] saw all humanity as created in God's image, as capable of *imitatio Christi* through body as well as soul. Thus they gloried in the pain, the exudings, the somatic distortions that made their bodies parallel to the consecrated wafer on the altar and the man on the cross." (p. 296)

4. After point twenty-nine in the defense of Antonio de la Peña the following passage, originally in Latin, appears in the text:

> "It appears from all this that there is so much excellence in the life and customs of the said Sor María and about her sanctimony and supernatural deeds that no scandal ought or should be taken. And if some scandalous son of perdition takes scandal, it was in the perniciousness of his own soul and not to mark this Sor María and her life, when they ought not understand or interpret all the deeds done through her except as good and sound, and thus it was and is by right."

5. Catherine of Siena, *The Dialogue,* tr. Suzanne Noffke, O.P. (New York: Paulist Press, 1980), p. 25.

6. Francisco de Osuna, *Third Spiritual Alphabet,* tr. Mary E. Giles (New York: Paulist Press, 1981), p. 315.

7. St. Teresa of Ávila, *Interior Castle,* p. 109.

8. St. Teresa of Ávila, *Interior Castle,* p. 214

9. St. John of the Cross, *Ascent of Mount Carmel,* tr. E. Allison Peers (Garden City, New York: Doubleday & Company, Inc., 1958), p. 93.

10. In Chapter XI of her autobiography, St. Teresa of Ávila describes the four ways of watering the garden of the soul:

> "It seems to me that the garden can be watered in four ways: by taking the water from a well, which costs us great labour; or by a water-wheel and buckets, when the water is drawn by a windlass (I have sometimes drawn it in this way: it is less laborious than the other and gives more water); or by a stream or a brook, which waters the ground much better, for it saturates it more thoroughly and there is less need to water it often, so that the gardener's labour

is much less; or by heavy rain, when the Lord waters it with no labour of ours, a way incomparably better than any of those which have been described."

St. Teresa of Ávila, *The Life of Teresa of Jesus,* tr. E. Allison Peers (Garden City, New York: Doubleday & Company, Inc., 1960), p. 128.

11. Catherine of Siena, *The Dialogue,* p. 60.

12. Elizabeth Alvilda Petroff, ed., *Medieval Women's Visionary Literature* (New York: Oxford University Press, 1986), p. 257.

13. Osuna, *Third Spiritual Alphabet,* p. 449.

14. Osuna, *Third Spiritual Alphabet,* p. 451.

15. St. Teresa of Ávila, *Interior Castle,* p. 175.

16. St. Teresa of Ávila, *Interior Castle,* pp. 171–72.

17. Elizabeth Alvilda Petroff says in the Introduction to *Medieval Women's Visionary Literature* that the narratives of these women exemplify "an autobiographical impulse, that is, a desire to put into words the search for what we would call a self—to express not just a formed and discovered self but to put into language the process of discovering and locating that self in relation to God, to the world, to others." (p. 22)

18. "Idem dico de scripturis meis quas dedi vestris dominationibus, quia ego prout ut in plurimum non scribebam quando ipsa loquebatur, sed audiebam, et forte una die et plus differebam commendare scripto quae memoriae commendaveram. Item quando eramus audientes duo aut tres aut decem, conferentes inter nos quid dixerit, unus sic et alius aliud dicebamus, ita quod non omnes eodem modo capiebant. Et propter hoc nolo dictis meis dare majorem fidem quam debeam." The entire document is included in Heredia's *Historia*, pp. 240–46.

19. From the Introduction to *The Dialogue,* p. 12.

20. From the Introduction to *The Dialogue,* p. 13.

21. From the Introduction to *The Dialogue,* p. 13.

22. From the Introduction to *The Dialogue,* p. 14.

23. Lillian S. Robinson, "Treason Our Text: Feminist Challenges to the Literary Canon" in *The New Feminist Criticism: Essays on Women, Literature, and Theory,* ed. Elaine Showalter (New York: Pantheon Books, 1985), p. 117.

24. Elaine Showalter, "Toward a Feminist Poetics" in *The New Feminist Criticism,* p. 131.

25. Annette Kolodny makes the case for pluralism in an altogether fascinating essay "Dancing Through the Minefield" in *The New Feminist Criticism,* pp. 144–67.

26. Richard B. Donovan, C.S.B., *The Liturgical Drama in Medieval Spain* (Toronto: Pontifical Institute of Medieval Studies, 1958), p. 49.

27. D. Fernando Lázaro Carreter, *Teatro Medieval* (Editorial Castalia, 1958), p. 32.

28. Translation of the selections from Gómez Manrique's play are by the author.

29. *Teatro completo de Juan del Encina,* ed. Francisco Asenjo Barbieri (Madrid, 1893; reprinted New York: Greenwood Press, 1969), p. xl.

30. Susan Gubar, "'The Blank Page' and the Issues of Female Creativity" in *The New Feminist Criticism,* p. 296.

31. Susan Gubar, "'The Blank Page'". p. 299.

32. Susan Gubar, "'The Blank Page'". p. 299.

33. From Annette Kolodny's "Dancing Through the Minefield" (p. 158): "To question the source of the aesthetic pleasures we have gained from reading Spenser, Shakespeare, Milton, and so on does not imply that we must deny those pleasures. It means only that aesthetic response is once more invested with epistemological, ethical, and moral concerns." And: "The pleasures we had earlier learned to take in the poem will not be diminished thereby, but they will become part of an altered reading attentiveness."

34. Susan Gubar, "'The Blank Page'". p. 296.

35. Sor María's text certainly calls for the kind of contextual study known as semiotics. The work of Julia Kristeva is especially insightful with respect to marginality in women and language. For a helpful introduction to French feminist theory with emphasis on

Hélène Cixous, Luce Irigaray and Julia Kristeva see Toril Moi, *Sexual/Textual Politics: Feminist Literary Theory* (London and New York: Routledge, 1985). See also Domna C. Stanton, "Difference on Trial: A Critique of the Maternal Metaphor in Cixous, Irigaray, and Kristeva" in *The Poetics of Gender,* ed. Nancy K. Miller (New York: Columbia University Press, 1986), pp. 157–82. The author cogently connects the semiotic and the maternal.

Conclusion

1.Osuna, *Third Spiritual Alphabet,* p. 47.

2. Bataillon, *Erasmo y España,* I, p. 81.

3. Márquez, *Los alumbrados,* p. 128.

4. Cited by Andrés in *La teología española,* p. 558.

5. Cited by Andrés in *La teología española,* p. 558.

6. Cited by Andrés in *La teología española,* p. 558.

7. In spite of Teresa's well-known self-depreciation on the grounds that she was an uneducated woman, there is a strong case made for her feminism. See Mary E. Giles, "The Feminist Mystic" in *The Feminist Mystic and Other Essays on Women and Spirituality,* ed. Mary E. Giles (New York: Crossroad Publishing Company, 1982; Mary E. Giles, "Teresa of Ávila and the Language of Ambiguity," unpublished paper.

8. Toril Moi, *Sexual/Textual Politics,* p. 167.

9. Toril Moi, *Sexual/Textual Politics,* p. 167.

The Book of Prayer

1. Born in Utrecht on March 2, 1459 Adrian Florensz took his doctorate in theology at Louvain in 1491 and rose to become chancellor of the university and tutor to the future Charles V. He went to Spain in 1515, acting as co-viceroy with Cardinal Cisneros after the death of King Ferdinand in 1516 and as sole viceroy after Cisneros died in 1517. In 1516 he was named bishop of Tortosa and inquisitor general of Aragon and Castile. A compromise candidate, he was elected to the papacy in 1522 and died the following year on September 12.

2. St. Anthony, born around 250 near Heracleopolis in Middle Egypt, is considered the founder of anchoretic life in Egypt, where it first flourished. After a long life of extreme penitence and exemplary holiness he died in 356.

3. Matt. 10:24. The disciple is not superior to his teacher, nor the slave to his master.

4. Luke 7:33–34. For John the Baptist comes, not eating bread, not drinking wine, and you say, "He is possessed". The Son of Man comes, eating and drinking, and you say, "Look, a glutton and a drunkard, a friend of tax collectors and sinners."

5. Paul, known as the Simple, left his wife when he was sixty years old to become one of St. Anthony's first disciples. He was honored for his humility and unwavering obedience. He died around 340 and his feast day is March seventh. St. Macarius the Great or the Elder, 300–390, spent sixty years in the desert of Scete, acquiring among the monks of Lower Egypt a reputation for wisdom and eloquence. St. Marcarius the Younger lived in the desert of the Cells in Lower Egypt. He died in 394. St. Hilarion, 291–372, was a disciple of St. Anthony who instituted monastic life in Palestine. He was said to have eaten only herbs and a small piece of bread each day. His feast day is October twenty-first. Serapion of Thmuis was also a friend of St. Anthony's who became a bishop and earned a reputation for scholarship as well as asceticism. He died after 362.

6. St. Apellen (spelled Appellen in the Spanish text) is a variant spelling of Ampelius who was a hermit in Thebaid where he served the brethren as a blacksmith. He moved to Italy where, after years of austere asceticism, he died on October 5, 428. His feast day is now May fourteenth.

7. St. Mary of Egypt was born around 354 in Northern Egypt. According to the legendary life which was written by Sophronius in the seventh century, she fled home at the age of twelve and was a prostitute in Alexandria for seventeen years. She was converted while she visited the Church of the Holy Sepulchre during a pilgrimage to Jerusalem. She did severe penance for over seventeen years and died in 422. Her feast was originally April second.

8. St. Nicholas of Flüe, 1417–1487, is the official patron saint of Switzerland. Although he was married with ten children, he left home at the age of fifty to establish an Alpine hermitage. He lived

as a recluse for twenty years, existing exclusively on the eucharist. He died on his seventieth birthday and was canonized in 1947.

9. Ecclesiasticus 11:28–30. Call no man fortunate before his death; it is by his end that a man will be known.

10. In the Spanish text the phrase is "llevar una culebra en la manga". A figurative meaning of "culebra" is a disturbance which a few people provoke in the midst of a peaceful gathering. Thus a person who carries a disturbance up his sleeve (llevar en la manga") could mean one who always disagrees with any idea or always is critical.

11. Matt. 12:22–32.

12. Dionysius the Pseudo-Areopagite was allegedly the disciple of St. Paul and the first bishop of Athens, but he is more commonly identified as a Syrian monk of the late fifth and early sixth centuries. In addition to *The Book of Divine Names* mentioned here, Dionysius is the author of *Mystical Theology* which strongly influenced medieval Christian mysticism in the theme of the *via negativa.*

13. St. Ignatius the Martyr was one of the most outstanding figures of the early Church. He may have been a disciple of St. Peter or St. Paul. He was condemned to the beasts in the games at Rome which were given by Trajan during the whole year of 107 to celebrate the success of his Dacian expedition.

14. Because the parish church in Aldeanueva was dedicated to Mary Magdalen, the monastery of Sor María also adopted the title. By 1512 Santa Cruz was added to the title; for the next twenty years or so the monastery was called either Santa Cruz de la Magdalena or Vera Cruz de la Magdalena. Almost all the religious had the name *María*. The community of religious continued in the house of Aldeanueva until 1872, when they were moved to the convent of Mosén Rubí in Ávila. (Heredia, *Historia,* p. 142.)

15. The passage reflects the spirit if not the exact wording of The Canticle of Canticles, 2:8–17.

16. José Subirá in his *Historia de la música española e hispanoamericana* (Barcelona: Salvat Editores, S.A., 1953) notes that the situation of keyboard instruments is puzzling in the early sixteenth century. The Spanish text identifies the instrument which Sor María was listening to as a *manacordio/clavicímbalo.*

The *manacordio*, which has variant spellings of *manocordio*, *monacordio* and *monicordio*, appears to be a clavichord. A *clavicímbalo* (or *clavicímbano*) was a clavichord whose strings were plucked. However, José Subirá makes it very clear that the *manacordio* was a clavichord whose strings were hammered. There may have been confusion on the part of the editor of *The Book of Prayer* which was the proper name for the instrument.

17. In the second half of the fourth century there spread throughout the Christian world the belief that the cross of Christ had been found and that pieces of it were in several places. In three of the four versions of the legend of the reappearance of the cross, Helena, the mother of Constantine, leads the way to the excavations either on her own volition or by divine inspiration. The Feast of the Discovery of the Cross traditionally was celebrated on May third; it was suppressed for the Latin rite in 1960.

18. The pearl, or as it is called "the pearl of great price," is a traditional image for the divine spark within each person.

Selected Bibliography

Andrés Martín, Melquíades. *El misterio de los alumbrados de Toledo, desvelado por sus contemporáneos (1523–1560).* Burgos, 1976.

———. *Nueva visión de los "alumbrados" de 1525.* Madrid: Fundación Universitaria Española, 1973.

———. *Los recogidos: nueva visión de la mística española (1500–1700).* Madrid: Fundación Universitaria Española, 1976.

———. *La teología española en el siglo XVI.* Vol. II. Madrid: La editorial católica, S.A., 1976.

Asenjo Barbieri, Francisco, ed. *Teatro completo de Juan del Encina.* Madrid, 1893; reprinted New York: Greenwood Press, 1969.

Bataillon, Marcel. *Erasmo y España.* 2 Vols. México-Buenos Aires: Fondo de Cultura Económica, 1950.

———. "Sur la diffusion des oeuvres de Savonarole en Espagne et en Portugal (1500–1560)," *Mélanges de philologie, d'histoire et de littérature offerts á Joseph Vianney.* Paris: Les Presses Françaises, 1934.

Bell, Rudolph M. *Holy Anorexia.* Chicago: The University of Chicago Press, 1985.

Beltrán de Heredia, Vicente. *Las corrientes de espiritualidad entre los dominicos de Castilla durante la primera mitad del siglo XVI.* Salamanca, 1941.

———. *Historia de la Reforma de la Provincia de España.* Rome, 1939.

———. *Miscelánea Beltrán de Heredia. Colección de artículos sobre historia de la teología española.* Vol. III. Salamanca: Biblioteca de teólogos españoles, 1972.

Bilinkoff, Jodi. "The Holy Woman and the Urban Community. Sixteenth-century Ávila" in *Women and the Structure of Society,* eds. Barbara J. Harris and JoAnn K. McNamara. Durham, North Carolina: Duke University Press, 1984.

Blecua, José Manuel, ed. *Libro de la Oración de Sor María de Santo Domingo.* Madrid: Hauser y Menet, 1948.

Bohmer, Edward. *Francisca Hernández y Frai Francisco Ortiz.* Leipzig: H. Haessel, 1865.

Bynum, Caroline Walker. *Holy Feast and Holy Fast. The Religious Significance of Food to Medieval Women.* Berkeley: University of California Press, 1987.

Catherine of Siena. *The Dialogue,* tr. Suzanne Noffke, O.P. New York: Paulist Press, 1980.

Cayré, F. *Manual of Patrology and History of Theology,* tr. H. Howitt. Vol. I. Paris, Tournai, Roma: Society of St. John the Evangelist, 1936.

Colunga, Emilio. "Intelectualistas y místicos en la teología española en el siglo XVI," *Ciencia tomista,* IX (1914), pp. 209–221 and pp. 377–394; X (1914–1915), pp. 223–242; XI (1915), pp. 237–252; XII (1915–1916), pp. 5–21.

Diccionario de Autoridades. Biblioteca Románica Hispánica. Madrid: Editorial Gredos, S.A., 1969.

Donovan, Richard B. *The Liturgical Drama in Medieval Spain.* Toronto: Pontifical Institute of Medieval Studies, 1958.

Dronke, Peter. *Women Writers of the Middle Ages. A Critical Study of Texts from Perpetua to Marguerite Porete.* Cambridge University Press, 1984.

Galíndez de Carvajal, Lorenzo. *Crónicas de los Reyes de Castilla.* Madrid: Biblioteca de Autores Españoles, 1953.

García de Oro, J. *Cisneros y la reforma del clero español en tiempos de los Reyes Católicos.* Madrid, 1971.

García Villoslada, Ricardo. *Historia de la iglesia en España.* 5 Vols. Madrid: La editorial católica, S.A., 1980.

Getino, L.A. *Vida ideario del maestro fray Pablo de León, verbo de las Comunidades castellanas.* Salamanca, 1935.

Giles, Mary E., ed. *The Feminist Mystic and Other Essays on Women and Spirituality.* New York: Crossroad Publishing Company, 1982.

Gougaud, Louis. *Devotional and Ascetic Practices in the Middle Ages.* London: Burns, Oates and Washbourne, 1927.

Holweck, Frederick George. *A Biographical Dictionary of the Saints.* St. Louis, Missouri and London: B. Herder Book Co., 1924.

Huerga, Álvaro. *Historia de los alumbrados.* 3 Vols. Madrid: Fundación Universitaria Española, 1978.

———. *Predicadores, alumbrados e Inquisidores en el siglo XVI.* Madrid: Fundación Universitaria Española, 1973.

Inmaculada, Román de la. "El fenómeno de los alumbrados y su interpretación," *Ephemerides Carmeliticae,* IX (1958), pp. 49–80.

St. John of the Cross. *Ascent of Mount Carmel.,* tr. E. Allison Peers Garden City, New York: Doubleday & Company, Inc., 1958.

Kamen, Henry. *Inquisition and Society in Spain in the Sixteenth and Seventeenth Centuries.* Bloomington, Indiana: Indiana University Press, 1985.

Kieckhefer, Richard. *Unquiet Souls: Fourteenth Century Saints and Their Religious Milieu.* Chicago: The University of Chicago Press, 1984.

Lafaye, Jacques. *Quetzalc*óatl and Guadalupe, tr. Benjamin Keen. Chicago and London: The University of Chicago Press, 1976.

Lázaro Carreter, Fernando. *Teatro Medieval.* Editorial Castalia, 1958.

Lea, Henry Charles. *History of the Inquisition of Spain.* 4 Vols. New York, 1906–1907.

———. *Inquisition of Spain.* Vol. IV. New York:AMS Press, Inc., 1966.

Longhurst, John E. "La beata Isabel de la Cruz ante la Inquisición," *Cuadernos de Historia de España,* 25–26 (1957), pp. 279–303.

Lunas Almeida, Jesús G. *Historia del Señorío de Valdecorneja en la parte referente a Piedrahita.* Ávila: Senén Martín, 1930.

Llorca, Bernardino. "Los alumbrados españoles en los siglos XVI y XVII," *Razón y Fe*, 105 (1934), pp. 323–342 and pp. 467–485.

———. "La beata de Piedrahita, ¿fué o no fué alumbrada?," *Manresa*, 1 (1942), pp. 46–62 and pp. 176–178; 16 (1944), pp. 275–285.

———. "Falsa doctrina sobre el abandono en los alumbrados," *Manresa*, 23 (1951), pp. 403–413.

———. *La inquisición española y los alumbrados (1509–1667)*. Salamanca: Universidad Pontífica, 1980.

Llorente, Juan Antonio. *Historia crítica de la Inquisición española*. Madrid, 1822.

Márquez, Antonio. *Los alumbrados. Orígenes y filosofía (1525–1559)*, 2nd ed. Madrid: Taurus Ediciones, S.A., 1980.

Márquez Villanueva, Francisco. *Literatura y espiritualidad en el siglo XVI*. Madrid: Alfaguara, 1968.

Menéndez Pelayo, Marcelino. *Historia de los heterodoxos españoles*. México: Editorial Porrúa, S.A., 1982.

Miller, Nancy K., ed. *The Poetics of Gender*. New York: Columbia University Press, 1986.

Moi, Toril *Sexual/Textual Politics: Feminist Literary Theory*. London and New York: Routledge, 1985.

Nieto José E. *Juan de Valdés and the Origins of the Spanish and Italian Reformation*. Genève: Droz, 1970.

Norton, F. J. A. *A Descriptive Catalogue of Printing in Spain and Portugal (1501–1520)*. Cambridge: Cambridge University Press.

Ortega Costa, Milagros. *Proceso de la Inquisición contra María de Cazalla*. Madrid: Fundación Universitaria Española, 1978.

Osuna, Francisco de. *Third Spiritual Alphabet*, tr. Mary E. Giles. New York: Paulist Press, 1981.

Pater, Thomas. *Miraculous Abstinence. A Study of One of the Extraordinary Mystical Phenomena*. Washington, D.C.: The Catholic University of America Press, 1946.

Petroff, Elizabeth Alvilda, ed. *Medieval Women's Visionary Literature*. New York: Oxford University Press, 1986.

Pou y Martí, J.M. *Visionarios, Beguinos y Fraticellos catalanes (siglos XII–XV).* Vich, 1930.

Rucquoi, Adeline. *Valladolid en la Edad Media.* Vol. II. Valladolid, 1987.

Selke de Sánchez, Ángela. "Algunos datos nuevos sobre los primeros alumbrados. El edicto de 1525 y su relación con el proceso de Alcaraz," *Bulletin Hispanique,* 54 (1952), pp. 125–152.

———. *El Santo Oficio de la Inquisición* Madrid: Guadarrama, 1968.

Serrano y Sanz, Manuel. *Apuntes para una biblioteca de escritoras españolas.* 2 Vols. Madrid, 1903–1905.

Showalter, Elaine, ed. *The New Feminist Criticism: Essays on Women, Literature and Theory.* New York: Pantheon Books, 1985.

Tapia, Ralph. *The Alumbrados of Toledo: A Study in Sixteenth Century Spanish Spirituality.* Park Falls, Wisconsin: Weber and Sons, Inc., 1974.

Tellechea, Idigoras, J. Ignacio. "Textos inéditos sobre el fenómeno de los alumbrados," *Ephemerides Carmeliticae,* 13 (1962), pp. 768–774.

Subirá, José. *Historia de la música española e hispano-americana.* Barcelona: Salvat Editores, S.A., 1953.

St. Teresa of Avila. *Interior Castle,* tr. E. Allison Peers. Garden City, New York: Doubleday & Company, Inc., 1961.

———. *The Life of Teresa of Jesus,* tr. E. Allison Peers. Garden City, New York: Doubleday & Company, Inc., 1960.

Thurston, Herbert. *The Physical Phenomena of Mysticism.* Chicago: Regnery, 1952.

Weinstein, Donald and Rudolph M. Bell. *Saints & Society. The Two Worlds of Western Christendom, 1000–1700.* Chicago and London: The University of Chicago Press, 1982.

Index